Celebrate Jesus!

AT EASTER

for

ASH WEDNESDAY

THROUGH EASTER

D0124158

Kimberly Ingalls Reese

CPH
SAINT LOUIS

Scripture quotations marked NRSV are from the New Revised Standard Version of the Bible, Copyright © 1989. Used by permission.

Scripture quotations, unless otherwise indicated, are taken from the HOLY BIBLE, NEW INTERNATIONAL VERSION®. NIV®. Copyright © 1973, 1978, 1984 by International Bible Society. Used by permission of Zondervan Publishing House. All rights reserved.

Copyright © 2002 Kimberly Ingalls Reese
Published by Concordia Publishing House
3558 S. Jefferson Avenue, St. Louis, MO 63118-3968
Manufactured in the United States of America

All rights reserved. No part of this publication may be reproduced, stored in a retrieval system, or transmitted, in any form or by any means, electronic, mechanical, photocopying, recording, or otherwise, without the prior written permission of Concordia Publishing House.

Library of Congress Cataloging-in-Publication Data

Reese, Kimberly Ingalls, 1960–
    Celebrate Jesus! at Easter : family devotions for Ash Wednesday through Easter / Kimberly Ingalls Reese.
      p. cm.
    ISBN 0-7586-0028-3
   1. Lent—Prayer -books and devotions—English. 2. Family—Prayer-books and devotions—English. I. Title.
    BV85 .R455 2002

242' .34—dc21
2001005842

1   2   3   4   5   6   7   8   9   10   11   10   09   08   07   06   05   04   03   02

This book is lovingly dedicated to my husband,
Dave, and our three children, Josiah, Samuel, and Sarah.
I give thanks to Jesus for blessing me with each one of you!

Table of Contents

These Devotions Are for You

You won't find any tales about bunnies here. Oh, I like bunnies—they're cute, they're fuzzy, they're adorable. But they have nothing whatsoever to do with the celebration of Easter. Easter is much greater than a cute bunny rabbit and its basket of chocolate eggs. Easter is a Christian's jubilee—our celebration of celebrations. It is the day we stand to proclaim that Jesus died, was buried, and has risen from the dead to save us.

As Christian parents, God gives us the mandate to teach what we know about Him to our children and to their children (Deuteronomy 6:7-8). We are to build traditions in our homes that will point them to their Redeemer and help them live lives of service to Him. What better opportunity than a holiday to build Bible truths into our children's lives? What better holiday than Easter?

Easter is one of my favorite times of the year, and I try to keep it as uncommercialized as possible. This is easier with Easter than it is with Christmas, although over the years the marketing of Easter paraphernalia has grown by leaps and bounds. With it, at best, comes the scrambling to fulfill wants and expectations that have nothing to do with Jesus' resurrection, and at worst it pulls our attention completely away from the One who saved our souls and brought us into fellowship with our Creator.

As Christians we must watch that secular attractions don't overshadow our celebration. Our children need to see firsthand the necessity of Jesus' death and resurrection, to know the certainty of God's unconditional love for them, and to learn to serve others in the power of that love.

Making the Most of Lent

Make the Lenten season special for you and for your family by setting aside time for daily devotions. The devotions offered in this book begin with Ash Wednesday and continue through Easter Sunday. Each one takes about fifteen minutes and is divided into five simple parts—prayer, Bible readings, discussion, singing, and hands-on service to God.

Take a few minutes to prepare by reading the devotions ahead of time. A list of materials for the suggested activities is given at the beginning of each week. Planning ahead and gathering the necessary items before they're needed will help prevent last-minute hassle that may distract from devotional time.

Remember, these are family devotions. Gather in a favorite room where everyone is comfortable. Every member of your family can participate in the praying, singing, reading, and serving. As each person participates, God's message becomes more meaningful to them. Give everyone a chance to lead a devotion. You'll be surprised how quickly a fidgety child can become an excited leader. We can all express praise and thankfulness to God for all He does through our Lord Jesus Christ.

Let's Live It is found at the beginning of each week and is full of practical applications to help everyone in your family put into action what you learn in devotions. Whether it is a family fast, dressing in first-century clothes and eating a simple supper, or helping at a local food bank, this section will show how faith affects life and the impact your faith has on people around you. But don't stop there. Invite your family to contribute faith application ideas of their own, write them in the spaces provided at the end of each **Let's Live It** section, then put them into practice.

$\mathcal{L}et's$ $\mathcal{P}ray$ offers a prayer to help your family focus on the theme of that day's devotion. Your family can personalize it to fit your needs and circumstances. Encourage your children to pray aloud during devotions. Even if they are just repeating the words you say, they are giving their praise and thanks to Jesus.

$\mathcal{R}eading$ provides selected Bible passages to read aloud. Vary the way passages are read. Have a different reader each night. Let each family member read one verse. Read the passage from different translations of the Bible (King James, Revised Standard, and New International versions, for example). Talk about what is being read. And be sure everyone understands the meaning of the passage. Make it exciting to hear God's Word. His truth changes our lives!

$\mathcal{T}hink$ $about$ $\mathcal{I}t$ provides questions and answers to use as a springboard for family discussions. Adapt the questions and answers to match your children's ages and levels of understanding.

$\mathcal{S}ing!$ is the time when your family gives praises to God. It can be as simple as raising your voices together or as elaborate as you want it to be. If members of your family play instruments, they can join right in. You can even make your own instruments! Then you can say right along with King David, "I will sing and make music with all my soul. Awake, harp and lyre! ... I will praise You, O LORD ..." (Psalm 108:1–3). If your children are very young, consider limiting the songs to one or two verses. If your family is not comfortable singing, read the songs aloud.

Activity Time is how the rubber of your faith can meet the road of your life. It is the time you can put into practice what you are learning and what you believe. Throughout His earthly ministry, Jesus served others. He taught them. He fed them. He loved them. And He calls all of us to follow in His footsteps. Talk with your family about ways to put your faith into action; the ideas here will get you started but the possibilities are endless. The Bible charges us to do everything with our whole heart working for God, not for man (Colossians 3:23).

You will also find three helpful appendices at the end of the book to enrich your family's worship during this wonderful season.

Ideas for Fasting is a list of many different ways your family can fast as a form of worship to God.

Teaching Your Children about the Resurrection gives ideas for explaining Jesus' resurrection to children. Our amazing Creator built much evidence into the natural world that points toward His plan for our redemption. The entire season of spring is devoted to rebirth and new beginnings; it is a great opportunity to share this spiritual truth with your children.

Hide It in Your Heart is a list of memory verses for Lent selected to coordinate with themes of the devotions included in this book. You can choose a verse for each week or choose one verse for the entire season. As we keep God's Word in our hearts, He uses it to work out His truth in our lives and in the lives of the people around us.

Celebrate Jesus! at Easter is a resource for building family togetherness. It is a tool for you to use as you learn God's Word, learn about Jesus' ministry on earth, and remember with thanksgiving all He has done. Share God's love with the world around you. Ask God to join in your Lenten preparations. Not only do we have His written Word, the Bible, to guide us in our understanding of Jesus, we have the Holy Spirit living inside us to testify of His love. Get ready to receive His abundant blessings!

Kimberly Ingalls Reese

What Is Lent Anyway?

*L*ent is the period before Easter Sunday that begins on Ash Wednesday and is 40 days long, not including Sundays. Lent is traditionally a time of reflection, repentance, and preparation for Easter, symbolizing Jesus' own time in the wilderness (Matthew 4:1–11). Sundays aren't included in Lent because Sundays are always a day for celebrating Jesus' resurrection.

In the early church, Lent was a time of preparation and learning for new converts who were baptized into the faith on Easter Sunday and then given new clothing. Their new clothing symbolized the forgiveness and new life Jesus brought them. This is where our tradition of wearing new clothes on Easter originates. As our families purchase or make special outfits for Easter, we can impress on our children the new life Jesus brings those who call upon His name.

Lent is a time of imitating Jesus' time in the wilderness. We can take a break from day-to-day living and think about what Jesus has done for us, what He means to us, and what we can do to share His love with others.

It is a time of practicing what God's Word teaches. In response to His gift of great love, we can pray for the people around us who don't know God's Good News and we can share His love with our words and actions as we give them our friendship and possibly meet some of their physical needs.

For many Christians, Lent is also a time of fasting. Fasting helps us identify with what Jesus endured for us on the cross. Nothing we do ourselves is truly comparable to what Jesus suffered, but fasting is a reminder that we were bought with a price. Our salvation cost Jesus dearly.

The Bible talks about fasting from food, but fasting doesn't have to be limited to giving up lunch on Wednesdays or not eating chocolate. Jesus called His followers to deny themselves in other ways too. Denying self is what fasting is really all about.

Fasting can be as simple as getting the clutter out of your life so you can focus more clearly on the Lord. Whether that means not eating certain foods or going without certain conveniences is up to you and your family to decide. The younger your children are, the shorter the fast can be. Maybe your family will decide to fast from TV on Wednesdays during Lent. Or maybe you can try a series of short fasts: a different one each week of Lent. (See **Ideas for Fasting** on page 150 for more.) Remember, no material thing can truly satisfy our souls' longing (Psalm 37:4, Matthew 11:28). We can take this opportunity to teach our children to not give in to personal desires but to look first at worshiping and serving their Creator.

Another opportunity we have during Lent is to serve or to give. We can give to others out of the great love we receive from Jesus. We can encourage our children to give time, money, and resources to help someone in need. Christmas is not the only time food banks or homeless shelters need donations. The needs of the hurting are never fully satisfied.

Whether your church officially observes Lent or your family quietly focuses your hearts on Jesus, the Lenten season is a significant time for teaching children about His life and ministry, His teaching, His suffering, and His death on the cross for our sins. Lent ends triumphantly on Easter Sunday when we rejoice in Jesus' victory over sin and death. His resurrection is the triumph.

As we pray and meditate on God's Word, we will be filled with His love. We will reaffirm our faith in Him and will be empowered by His Spirit to do His work in the lives of others. We will have the strength to say no to our self-centered desires and yes to God-centered ones.

> My son, do not forget my teaching, but keep my commands in your heart, for they will prolong your life many years and bring you prosperity. Let love and faithfulness never leave you; bind them around your neck, write them on the tablet of your heart. ... In all your ways acknowledge Him, and He will make your paths straight. Proverbs 3:1–3, 6

The Beginning of Lent:
Ash Wednesday—In the Wilderness

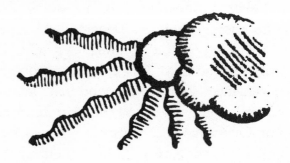

At once the spirit sent Him out into the desert,

and He was in the desert forty days.

Mark 1:12—13a

Here we are at the beginning of Lent. Lent is the 40-day period before our celebration of Easter Sunday. It is a time of reflection, for remembering what Jesus did for us. It is a time of learning and discovering more about who Jesus is and what He wants us to do. It is a time of giving and serving in Jesus' name.

Materials Needed This Week

Holy Bible

Household items or toys to use as armor of God

Construction paper

Old magazines

Clear adhesive vinyl

Construction paper for family seal

Let's Live It

1. Begin talking as a family about what kind of fasting you want to do. See **Ideas for Fasting** on page 150.

2. Try having a "wilderness day". Ask your family to withdraw from your normal schedule of events to spend time together. Sometime during the day read the Bible and pray together. Talk about Jesus' time in the wilderness. Not only did He stand firm against Satan, He spent time with God the Father. We can draw closer to God, too, and learn how He wants us to serve Him.

3. Agree to learn a Bible verse together each week of Lent. See **Hide It in Your Heart** on page 154 for ideas. If your children are very young, choose just one Bible verse to learn during Lent.

4. Pray each day at dinnertime for friends and family who don't know that Jesus loves them. Pray that they might recognize His love this Lenten season.

5. Make a living Easter basket. Put potting soil in a small container and sprinkle grass seed on top. Gently add water. Tend it until you have a full basket of grass, then fill it with little treats and give it to someone special.

6.

7.

Ash Wednesday

Let's Pray

Dear Lord God, open our hearts and minds today as we learn together from Your Holy Word. In the name of Jesus, our Savior. Amen.

Reading

Matthew 4:1-11

Think about It

Temptation is a big word; what does it mean? If someone is being tempted, they are faced with a choice between doing something wrong and resisting the urge. They could be tempted to say something that is hurtful or untrue. They could be tempted to do something wrong, like pushing all their toys under the bed when Mom has asked them to clean their room. Or they could be tempted to not do something good, like taking out the trash without being asked to.

Right after John baptized Jesus, Jesus went into the wilderness by Himself. The Bible says that the Holy Spirit led Him away to be alone with God so He could get ready to begin His public ministry. While Jesus was alone, Satan came and tempted Him three times.

What were the ways Jesus was tempted? First Jesus was fasting, so He was very hungry. Satan tempted Him with food. He said that since Jesus was the Son of God, He could turn rocks into bread. Second, the devil tempted Jesus with physical safety. He took Jesus to the top of a mountain and told Him to test God by jumping off. Then Satan offered Jesus an easy way to be very rich and powerful and be king of the world. Jesus didn't listen to Satan. He knew that God's way is always best. Although going without food and turning down riches was the harder path, He chose to obey God and resist temptation.

Why did God allow Jesus to be tempted? Jesus was tempted so He could understand us and the temptations we face each day. Whether you are a student who faces the problems of classmates, homework, and obeying your parents, or you're a parent who faces the working world, managing a home, and raising a godly family, Jesus understands your problems and He cares about you.

How did Jesus resist the temptations? Jesus fought against those temptations with God's Holy Word, the Bible. That is where we turn for the answers to our struggles as well. God gave us His Word to show us what sin is and to help us fight against it. The Bible says God will never let us be tempted by more than we can resist (1 Corinthians 10:13). Jesus is ready, willing, and able to help any time we ask—day or night. With Jesus, we can face anything!

Let's Pray

Dear Lord Jesus, we are tempted every day in many ways. We can choose to follow You or to give in to temptations. It is so good to know that You understand our temptations and how hard it is to resist. Help us to choose Your way. Thank You for always being there to help us. In Your name. Amen.

Activity Time

Think of a temptation you have. Share it with one another and talk about ways you can stand against it. The Bible says to stand firm and resist Satan (1 Peter 5:9). Can you find other verses that help your situation? Encourage one another.

Sing!

A Mighty Fortress Is Our God

Martin Luther, 1483–1546
Tr. composite

EIN FESTE BURG
Martin Luther, 1483–1546

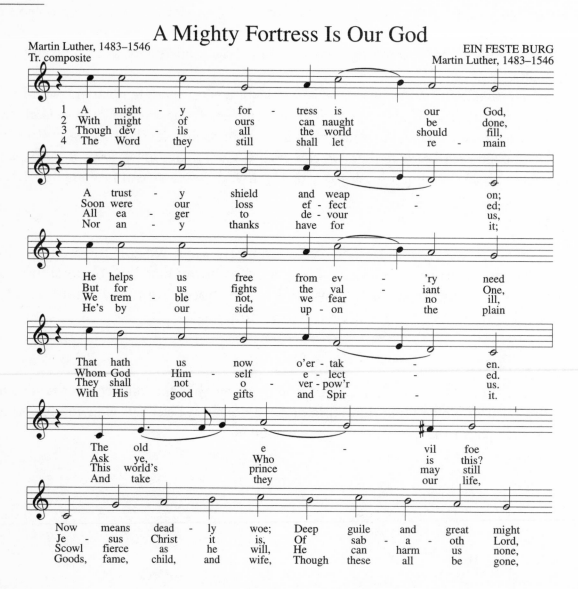

1 A might - y for - tress is our God,
2 With might of ours can naught be done,
3 Though dev - ils all the world should fill,
4 The Word they still shall let re - main

A trust - y shield and weap - on;
Soon were our loss ef - fect - ed;
All ea - ger to de - vour us,
Nor an - y thanks have for it;

He helps us free from ev - 'ry need
But for us fights the val - iant One,
We trem - ble not, we fear no ill,
He's by our side up - on the plain

That hath us now o'er - tak - en.
Whom God Him - self e - lect - ed.
They shall not o - ver - pow'r us.
With His good gifts and Spir - it.

The old e - vil foe
Ask ye, Who is this?
This world's prince may still
And take they our life,

Now means dead - ly woe; Deep guile and great might
Je - sus Christ it is, Of sab - a - oth Lord,
Scowl fierce as he will, He can harm us none,
Goods, fame, child, and wife, Though these all be gone,

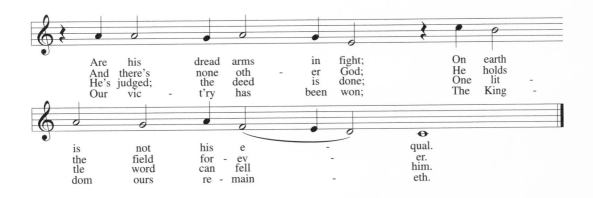

Are   his   dread   arms   in   fight;   On   earth
And   there's   none   oth - er   God;   He   holds
He's   judged;   the   deed   is   done;   One   lit -
Our   vic - t'ry   has   been   won;   The   King -

is   not   his   e -   qual.
the   field   for - ev -   er.
tle   word   can   fell   him.
dom   ours   re - main -   eth.

Thursday after Ash Wednesday

Let's Pray

Dear heavenly Father, we thank You that You are always
ready to help us overcome any problems in our life.
In the name of Your Son, Jesus. Amen.

Reading

Hebrews 4:14–16

19

Think about It

What does the Bible mean when it says in Hebrews 4:14 that Jesus is our great, high priest? In the Old Testament, priests went to God with sacrifices and asked Him to forgive people's sins. Things changed for God's people when Jesus came. He stands before God, our heavenly Father, and acts as our priest. He made atonement, or payment, for our sins with His death on the cross. When we confess Jesus as our Savior and believe in His work on the cross, He is our heavenly priest. Jesus is also our sacrifice. Our sins are forgiven because Jesus sacrificed Himself on our behalf.

How can Jesus sympathize with or have understanding for the things we struggle with? According to Hebrews 4:15, He understands our problems because He was tempted Himself. When Jesus was on earth, He was a human being who was faced with all the things we struggle with—being honest, being obedient, working hard, being a good friend. In other words, in every common way that we are tempted, Jesus was also tempted. But Jesus didn't give in to temptation even once. He can help us to not give in either.

What are some of the things you struggle with? Maybe you struggle with speaking kindly to a brother or sister. Maybe it's hard to be patient while you wait for others to help you. Maybe it seems easier to lie than to tell the truth when you are in a tough spot. Everyone has things in their lives they struggle with, ways they are tempted to disobey God's laws. The Bible says no one is perfect. Not one person. Even if they look perfect on the outside, God sees their heart (Matthew 15:18–19; Romans 3:23). Share a struggle you each have and talk about how Jesus would want you to act.

Now that we've thought about and shared some sin struggles in our lives, what can we do about them? God has given us a way to receive forgiveness for our sins and to help us resist sin in the future through His Son, Jesus. Look at Hebrews 4:16. We do not have to be alone in our struggles. We can go to Jesus. The verse says draw near to the throne of grace. Tell Jesus what is happening in your life. Confess to Him how you have disobeyed His Word, and ask for His forgiveness. He will always forgive you (Psalm 103:10–13; James 1:9). Our sin is covered by His grace (Psalm 32:1). We don't have to be afraid or shy about bringing temptations or struggles to Him in prayer. He cares about us (1 Peter 5:7). In fact, when we pray about our problems, Jesus has promised to help us (Matthew 11:28).

Sing!

What a Friend We Have in Jesus

CONVERSE

Joseph Scriven, 1820–86

Charles C. Converse, 1832–1918

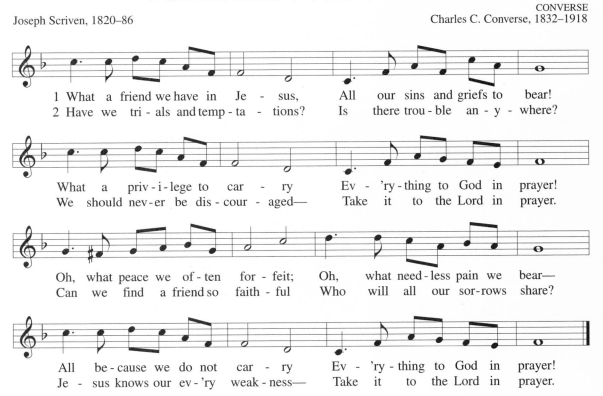

1 What a friend we have in Je - sus, All our sins and griefs to bear!
2 Have we tri - als and temp - ta - tions? Is there trou - ble an - y - where?

What a priv - i - lege to car - ry Ev - 'ry - thing to God in prayer!
We should nev - er be dis - cour - aged— Take it to the Lord in prayer.

Oh, what peace we of - ten for - feit; Oh, what need - less pain we bear—
Can we find a friend so faith - ful Who will all our sor - rows share?

All be - cause we do not car - ry Ev - 'ry - thing to God in prayer!
Je - sus knows our ev - 'ry weak - ness— Take it to the Lord in prayer.

Let's Pray

Lord Jesus, We thank You that You are always here to help us no matter what happens in our lives. We thank you that You loved us enough to come to earth and die for our sins. Help us to follow Your example and to be quick to ask for Your help. We pray these things in Your name. Amen.

Activity Time

Read Ephesians 6:10–18. This is God's prescription to help us fight temptation. Find these items around your house and dress up in the armor of God. You'll need a belt, a breastplate (maybe a vest), shoes, a shield (the lid from a toy box works well), a helmet (a cap or hat), and a sword. Be creative and learn together what protection God gives us to stand firm.

Friday after Ash Wednesday

Let's Pray

Dear God, we love You and want to follow You better. Help us to listen to Your Word, the Bible, and live out what it says. For Jesus' sake. Amen.

Reading

Matthew 3:1–12

Think about It

John the Baptist was God's prophet. A prophet was a special leader chosen by God. John moved from place to place to talk to the Jewish people about God. He was calling them back to God. Urging them to get to know God better. God sent him to get the people ready to hear the teachings of Jesus. He baptized people who were sorry for their sins and for not loving God. These people wanted to come back to God's love.

What does the word "repent" mean? When someone repents, they know that something they have been doing, saying, or thinking is wrong and doesn't please God. They stop this behavior and ask God to forgive them. They ask Him to help them to do a better job of following Him. The Bible says, "Turn from evil and do good" (Psalm 34:14; 37:27).

Do we need to repent? Yes we do. We cannot go even one day without sinning. And every time we sin, we turn away from God. When we repent, we turn back to God, telling Him we are sorry for our sins. God's Good News is that He forgives us each and every time because Jesus died for our sins on the cross.

What made John talk to the Pharisees and Sadducees like he did? The Pharisees and Sadducees were leaders in the Jewish community. They were proud about looking spiritual. They didn't think they needed to turn away from their sin. In fact, they thought they didn't sin at all. But these men didn't fool John or God. Everyone, even the Pharisees and Sadducees, has sinned and comes short of the glory of God (Romans 3:23). It is only by God's grace that we are saved (Acts 15:11; Ephesians 2:5).

Sing!

Glory Be to Jesus

Italian, 18th cent.
Tr. Edward Caswall, 1814–78

WEM IN LEIDENSTAGEN
Friedrich Filitz, 1804–76

1 Glo - ry be to Je - sus, Who in bit - ter pains
2 Grace and life e - ter - nal In that blood I find;
3 Blest through end - less a - ges Be the pre - cious stream
4 A - bel's blood for ven - geance Plead - ed to the skies;

Poured for me the life - blood From His sa - cred veins.
Blest be His com - pas - sion, In - fi - nite - ly kind.
Which from end - less tor - ment Did the world re - deem.
But the blood of Je - sus For our par - don cries.

5 Oft as earth exulting
 Wafts its praise on high,
Angel hosts rejoicing
 Make their glad reply.

6 Lift we then our voices,
 Swell the mighty flood;
Louder still and louder
 Praise the precious blood.

23

Let's Pray

Dear Jesus, we are sorry for any bad things we did or said or thought about today. Please forgive us and make us clean on the inside. Remind us that we are baptized in Your name. We thank You that You have the power to do that! Amen.

Activity Time

Make placemats that show the armor of God to use during Lent. Cut out pictures from old magazines or draw your own. Glue the pictures onto a large piece of construction paper and laminate it or cover the whole piece of paper with clear adhesive vinyl. Now you have a visual reminder of God's protection against temptation. Remember to thank God for His protection when you say mealtime prayers.

Saturday/Sunday after Ash Wednesday

Let's Pray

Dear Lord Jesus, You have always been obedient to Your Father. Thank You for setting a good example for us to follow. Help us to be obedient too. In Your name we pray. Amen.

Reading

Matthew 3:13–17

Think about It

Day after day, John was faithful to what God told him to do. He baptized people who were sorry for their sins and got them ready to hear Jesus' teaching. John knew who Jesus was. He knew Jesus was God's Son and did not need to repent. Yet Jesus was obedient to His Father, so He came to John to be baptized too. God the Father showed His love for Jesus in a very special way. He sent the Holy Spirit as a dove to make Jesus ready for His work on earth.

Read verses 13–15 again. *Did Jesus need to be baptized?* At first John did not think so. John knew that Jesus was God's Son and that He had never sinned. In fact John called out, "Behold the Lamb of God who takes away the sin of the world" (John 1:29). John may have thought that since Jesus had never sinned, He didn't need to repent or to be baptized.

Yet Jesus came to be baptized to show that He was our substitute, that He was going to take our sins to the cross. And the waters of our own Baptism show us that our sins have been washed away and our hearts have been cleansed because of what Jesus did for us on the cross.

What special thing happened at Jesus' Baptism? The Holy Spirit, in the form of a dove, came down from heaven to Jesus. God set Him apart from the people around Him for the special work He was going to do. This special work led Jesus to death and resurrection.

Does God set other people apart like this? The seal of the Holy Spirit sets us all apart (Ephesians 1:13). God knows us and has created us to serve Him in unique ways. Pastors and missionaries are set apart for the special work they do as they follow God's direction for their lives. But there is only one Jesus, and no one else can save people from their sin.

Let's Pray

Jesus, You are amazing. Thank You for being such a clear example to us. Help us to be obedient to the Father even as You are always obedient. Thank You for sealing each of us with Your Holy Spirit, who helps us do Your will. In Your holy name. Amen.

Activity Time

There are many kinds of seals: seals on legal papers, seals on letters, agreements sealed with a handshake. Today make a family seal. Think of a motto to go across your seal. It could be a Bible verse, a common saying, or just one word that describes your family. Divide your seal into four sections and draw a picture in each section: one showing a hobby, one showing an activity you all enjoy, one showing the most important thing in your lives, one showing a goal your family has. When your seal is finished, put it in a prominent place in your home so everyone can see it.

Sing!

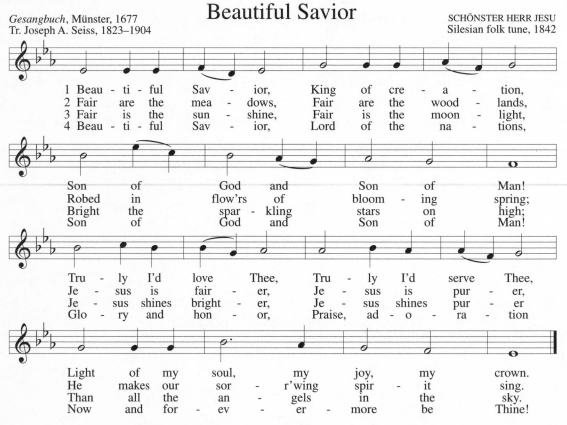

Beautiful Savior

Gesangbuch, Münster, 1677
Tr. Joseph A. Seiss, 1823–1904

SCHÖNSTER HERR JESU
Silesian folk tune, 1842

1 Beau - ti - ful Sav - ior, King of cre - a - tion,
2 Fair are the mea - dows, Fair are the wood - lands,
3 Fair is the sun - shine, Fair is the moon - light,
4 Beau - ti - ful Sav - ior, Lord of the na - tions,

Son of God and Son of Man!
Robed in flow'rs of bloom - ing spring;
Bright the spar - kling stars on high;
Son of God and Son of Man!

Tru - ly I'd love Thee, Tru - ly I'd serve Thee,
Je - sus is fair - er, Je - sus is pur - er,
Je - sus shines bright - er, Je - sus shines pur - er
Glo - ry and hon - or, Praise, ad - o - ra - tion

Light of my soul, my joy, my crown.
He makes our sor - r'wing spir - it sing.
Than all the an - gels in the sky.
Now and for - ev - er - more be Thine!

26

Second Week of Lent: Believing in Who Jesus Is

For God so loved the world that He gave His one and only Son, that whoever believes in Him shall not perish but have eternal life.

John 3:16

This week we will look at who Jesus is: who He said He was and who God said He was. Jesus is by nature God. He is also by nature human. The Bible calls Him both the Son of God and the Son of Man. That puts Jesus in the very unique position of being our heavenly priest. He is the only one who can bring us out of sin and back into a relationship with God, the Father. The pressure is taken off of us. We don't do anything but grab hold in faith to what Christ has done for us. He has done all the work.

Materials Needed This Week

Holy Bible
Basket of some type
Bottle of water
Lamb figurine
Candle
Loaf of bread
Map
Bible or Bible storybook
Note from your family about what Jesus means to you

    This week your family can make a "Who Is Jesus?" basket. You will add one item to the basket at the end of each day's devotion. Use this basket to decorate your home this Lenten season or give it to bless someone who might need to be reminded of Jesus' love for them.

Let's Live It

1. Talk with your children about the Holy Trinity. It's a difficult concept to explain, but you can do it! Try using these examples. None perfectly describe the Trinity, but they will give your children something to visualize.

    a. Show them a pencil and talk about its parts. The eraser, wooden outside, and lead, are all parts of the pencil. A pencil really isn't a pencil without all parts working together. Three parts but one pencil.

    b. Talk about the three forms of water: liquid, solid, and gas. Three forms but always water.

    c. Look at an egg. It has three distinct parts—shell, yolk, and white. It takes all three parts to make the egg. Three parts but one egg.

    d. Father, Son, and Holy Spirit. Three Persons but one God.

2. Just before you go to church, talk about why the worship service is conducted the way it is. It is focused around the person of Jesus Christ. It is only because of Him that we can call ourselves children of God. Jesus is the only way we get to heaven.

3. Parents, talk about your faith with your children. Tell why being a Christian is important to you.

4. Fast together as a family. Spend extra time reading His Word and praying.

5. Plant flower seeds this week to get blooms by Easter. See **Teaching Your Children about the Resurrection** on page 152 for this and other ideas.

6.

7.

Monday of the Second Week

Let's Pray

Thank You, Lord God, that You sent Jesus to earth. Thank You for showing Mary and Joseph and Simeon and Anna so clearly who Jesus was and what His mission would be. In Jesus' holy name. Amen.

Reading

Luke 2:21–40

Think about It

God's presence with Jesus was seen from the very beginning of His earthly life. God's angel came to Mary and Joseph before He was born. More angels proclaimed His birth to the shepherds. When Jesus was brought to the temple, according to Jewish custom, God spoke through Simeon and Anna. Jesus is the promised Messiah, the One everyone was waiting for. He is special. His life is special. Jesus is God's pathway for our salvation.

Who was Simeon? The Bible says he was a righteous and devout man. This means he loved, served, and obeyed the Lord. God had promised Simeon that he would see the Messiah before he died. Anna was a prophetess. She was very old. Anna worshiped, prayed, and fasted all day and night. She never left the temple.

What did Anna do when she saw Jesus? What did Simeon do? They praised God for being faithful and they blessed the baby Jesus. Giving a blessing to Jewish babies when they were brought to the temple was a common practice. But this blessing was different. It told who Jesus really was and what He was going to do here on earth.

What was Mary and Joseph's response? The Bible says they marveled at what was said. Everything that was happening in their lives was so incredible—unbelievable—that they were speechless. They didn't understand everything that had happened or that would happen in their family, but they loved God very much and wanted to follow Him.

Sing!

God Loves Me Dearly

August Rische 19th cent.
Tr. composite

GOTT IST DIE LIEBE
German folk tune

1 God loves me dear - ly, Grants me sal -
2 I was in slav - 'ry, Sin, death, and
3 He sent forth Je - sus, My dear Re -
4 Je - sus, my Sav - ior, Him - self did

va - tion, God loves me dear - ly, Loves e - ven me.
dark - ness; God's love was work - ing To make me free.
deem - er, He sent forth Je - sus And set me free.
of - fer; Je - sus, my Sav - ior, Paid all I owed.

Refrain

There - fore I'll say a - gain: God loves me

dear - ly, God loves me dear - ly, Loves e - ven me.

5 Now I will praise You,
O Love Eternal;
Now I will praise You
All my life long. *Refrain*

Let's Pray

Dear heavenly Father, it is so loving how You told Mary and Joseph that Jesus was special and His time on earth would be special. Thank You, Lord God, for loving people so much that You carefully planned and carried out our salvation through Your Son. We pray this in the name of Jesus, the Savior You sent us. Amen.

Activity Time

Add a bottle of water to the basket. Jesus brought us living water. That water is God's abundant and eternal life for all who believe (John 4:10–14, John 7:37–38, Revelation 21:6).

Tuesday of the Second Week

Let's Pray

Thank You, Jesus, because each day we have to know You is a great gift. Thank You for Your gift of life, which is free to all those who believe. Thank You for Your gift of love, which is always ours no matter what happens. In Your name we pray. Amen.

Reading

Isaiah 53:5–7 and 1 Peter 1:18–21

Think about It

Everyone knows that when we disobey the rules at home or school, there are consequences. The same thing is true with God. When His laws are broken, there are consequences.

In the Old Testament, a perfect lamb was given to God to pay for a person's or a family's sin (Leviticus 4:33; 5:6). The lamb was taken to the temple and killed in the place of that person or family. Then that person was at peace with God. He was a friend with God. This had to be done over and over because people sinned over and over. *We don't kill lambs now, so how can we be friends with God?*

Jesus is the Lamb of God. The Bible says this in many places (John 1:29). He took the punishment for all the bad things we say, think, and do. *What does the "Lamb of God" mean?*

Jesus is God's perfect lamb. When He died on the cross, He took care of everyone's sin forever. No other sacrifice ever has to be made. 1 Peter 1:21 says that our belief, faith, and hope in God through our Savior Jesus is all we need.

If we had to pay for our sins ourselves, the punishment would never end. Jesus took all the punishment we deserve—all the time outs, groundings, and penalties. Jesus wanted to stand in for us so we could be friends with God. *Did Jesus decide to do this on His own because He was a really good man?* No! The Bible tells us that Jesus is God's own Son. He is God. The Father sent Jesus into this world on a mission. From Adam and Eve down to us, human beings have messed up their lives by disobeying God. We have messed up so much that only God Himself can help us out of it. He knew this would happen from the beginning of time (1 Peter 1:20). Because He loved us so much, He gave us that way out: Jesus.

Look at the description in Isaiah 53. *What was it like to be the Lamb of God?* Stabbed. Crushed. Punished. Beaten. Oppressed. Afflicted. It was not fun and games. Jesus felt all of the pain that comes from disobeying God. He felt all of the sadness of being separated from God. He felt it so we would not have to. Only Someone who loves us with an everlasting love would do that.

Let's Pray

Precious Lord Jesus, how can we even begin to say thank You for all You have done and continue to do in our lives. How wonderful it is to know all we need is to believe in You. You are awesome! Amen.

Sing!

Just as I Am

Charlotte Elliott, 1789–1871

WOODWORTH
William B. Bradbury, 1816–68

1 Just as I am, with - out one plea But
2 Just as I am and wait - ing not To
3 Just as I am, though tossed a - bout With
4 Just as I am, poor, wretch - ed, blind; Sight,
5 Just as I am, Thou wilt re - ceive, Wilt
6 Just as I am; Thy love un - known Has

that Thy blood was shed for me And that Thou bidd'st me
rid my soul of one dark blot, To Thee, whose blood can
man - ya con - flict, man - ya doubt, Fight - ings and fears with -
rich - es, heal - ing of the mind, Yea, all I need, in
wel - come, par - don, cleanse, re - lieve; Be - cause Thy prom - ise
bro - ken ev - 'ry bar - rier down; Now to be Thine, yea,

come to Thee,
cleanse each spot,
in, with - out, O Lamb of God, I come, I come.
Thee to find,
I be - lieve,
Thine a - lone,

Activity Time

Add a lamb figurine to the basket. Jesus was God's perfect lamb, sacrificed in our place. He was punished so we don't have to be eternally punished (Genesis 22:8; Isaiah 53:7; Revelation 5:12).

Wednesday of the Second Week

Let's Pray

Father God, thank You that You have taken care of everything to make sure we know who Jesus is and what He has done for us. In Your Son's name. Amen.

Reading

Matthew 3:17, 17:1–8 and John 3:16

Think about It

Jesus is God's Son. This fact is so important. God didn't want us to miss it so He said it Himself, "This is My beloved Son, in whom I am well pleased" (Matthew 3:17 NKJV). God makes His Good News very clear. Everyone can hear it. God's love for us is so great that He actually sent His Son to suffer in our place so we can be friends with Him. Amazing isn't it?

Did Jesus know what was going to happen when He and His close friends went up on the mountain? Yes, remember Jesus is God's Son. He knows everything. It was in God's plan for Peter, James, and John to hear these words. It is through their faithfulness that we hear them too.

What exactly happened to Jesus on that mountain (Matthew 17:2–3)? Jesus was transfigured. His true, spiritual self was uncovered so there would be no doubt about who He was. Jesus is God's own Son sent to earth on a mission. Jesus' face shined like the sun, light was pouring out of Him. His clothing glowed with spiritual light that comes only from God. Jesus was not just a man. He is God.

What four things did God say on that mountain? The words God spoke are saved in His Word, the Bible, for us to hear today. Everything He said then is true now: Jesus is His Son. God loves Jesus. God is pleased with Jesus. And we are to listen to (or obey) what Jesus says.

Why was it important for Peter, James, and John to see Jesus' transfiguration and hear God's words? Peter, James, and John were witnesses. They witnessed both Jesus' heavenly glory and they witnessed His cruel death. Later they each remembered what they saw and they told others about it. This led other people to believe in Jesus and receive forgiveness for their sins. We can be witnesses too.

Sing!

Praise God, from Whom All Blessings Flow

Thomas Ken, 1637–1711

OLD HUNDREDTH
Louis Bourgeois, c. 1510–c. 1561

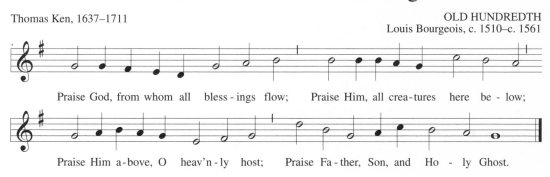

Praise God, from whom all bless-ings flow; Praise Him, all crea-tures here be-low;

Praise Him a-bove, O heav'n-ly host; Praise Fa-ther, Son, and Ho-ly Ghost.

Let's Pray

Lord Jesus, can there be any doubt? You are God. You are holy. You are light. You are awesome. Like Peter, James, and John, we bow down and worship You. Amen.

Activity Time

Add a candle to the basket. Jesus is the Light of the world. He lights our path while we walk on earth and He will light our way in heaven (Isaiah 9:2; John 8:12; 1 John 1:5–7; Revelation 22:5).

Thursday of the Second Week

Let's Pray

We praise You, Father God, for sending us Jesus. He is our only way to be friends with You. We praise You for sending Him to be our Savior. In Jesus' name. Amen.

Reading

Hebrews 7:24–27, 10:19–23

Think about It

Jesus is God's new and living way for us to communicate with Him. He is God's priest or agent. An agent is someone who has been given special power to act in place of someone very important. Jesus is our friend and acts for our good. He shows us the way to friendship with God. We can come close to God without being afraid that He won't like us. We can come close to God because of what Jesus has done for us and because of our faith in Him.

How is Jesus our high priest? Jesus is everything a priest is supposed to be. He is holy, blameless, and pure. He goes to God the Father for us. He gave His very life so we might be alive in God, so we might have a friendship with God. No more sacrifices are needed; He is the sacrifice. Jesus teaches us how to live, and He heals our pain. We are God's children because of Him.

How is Jesus' priesthood different from our pastor's ministry? Only Jesus can offer the sacrifice for our sin on the cross—Himself. He is the High Priest and the sacrifice itself. Pastors cannot offer sacrifices for sin because there is only one sacrifice for sin. However, they can and do announce that our sins are forgiven for Christ's sake and in His name. They do this as they preach God's Word, baptize new believers, announce God's forgiveness for Jesus' sake in absolution, and present Jesus to us in the Lord's Supper.

The Bible says we can draw near to God with a sincere heart and assurance of faith. *What does that mean?* Another way to say it is that we can come before God, tell the truth about our sin, and know (have the assurance of faith) that He forgives us because Jesus has taken care of our punishment. God sees our sin. He judges it and accepts Jesus' sacrifice for it. We are clean.

Will Jesus' sacrifice be enough? Absolutely! Jesus' sacrifice was good yesterday, today, and tomorrow. He is the perfect lamb. His promise to bring us to God is faithful. It lasts forever. All we have to do is believe it.

Let's Pray

Lord Jesus, it is so good to know we don't have to hide our sin from You. We have fallen short of Your glory. We have done things that are wrong. Please forgive us. Clean our hearts, and help us to follow You. In Your name we pray. Amen.

Activity Time

Add bread to the basket. Jesus called Himself the bread of life. Just as we need physical food to live and be healthy, we need Jesus to be spiritually healthy (Deuteronomy 8:3; Matthew 4:4; Matthew 6:11; John 6:35).

Sing!

Amazing Grace

John Newton, 1725–1807, alt.

NEW BRITAIN
J. Carrell and D. Clayton, *Virginia Harmony*, 1831

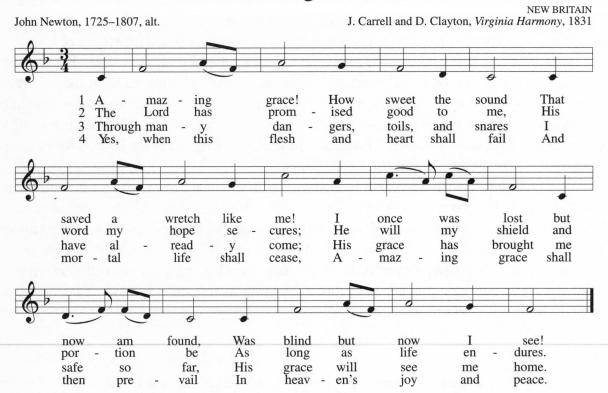

1 A - maz - ing grace! How sweet the sound That
2 The Lord has prom - ised good to me, His
3 Through man - y dan - gers, toils, and snares I
4 Yes, when this flesh and heart shall fail And

saved a wretch like me! I once was lost but
word my hope se - cures; He will my shield and
have al - read - y come; His grace has brought me
mor - tal life shall cease, A - maz - ing grace shall

now am found, Was blind but now I see!
por - tion be As long as life en - dures.
safe so far, His grace will see me home.
then pre - vail In heav - en's joy and peace.

40

Friday of the Second Week

Let's Pray

We praise You, Jesus, for all that You are—fully God and fully human. You are the answer to all we need. In Your name. Amen.

Reading

John 1:1–5, 10–14

Think about It

We learned from other devotions that when Jesus came to earth, He became a human being like us. He understands our problems, our temptations, and our struggles. But there is another side to Jesus, and that is His God nature. He is God and has existed forever. He came to earth on a divine mission to help us become children of God.

Did Jesus' life begin in the manger in Bethlehem? Jesus' earthly life started in Bethlehem, but Jesus has always existed (John 1:1–3). People were so trapped in their sins they had no hope of escaping. No one could go even one day without sinning, let alone a lifetime. It was so hopeless that God Himself had to come to earth to set us free.

The Bible says that Jesus had life and that life was the light of men. *What does that mean to us?* Just like a lighthouse helps the sailor avoid dangerous rocks and find safe harbor, Jesus' love shines through our sin to bring us God's love and forgiveness. Jesus gives us hope. Through Him, we can escape the sin we are in.

How do we become children of God? The Bible says that as many as believe in His name He will make children of God. Jesus has done all the work. He came to earth. He taught us God's truth. He died on the cross to set us free. He makes us His own through the power of His Word and the waters of Baptism.

Sing!

I've Got the Joy

Traditional

Traditional

1 I've got the joy,— joy,— joy,— joy— down in my heart,
2 I've got the love of Je-sus, love of Je-sus down in my heart,
3 I've got the peace that pass-es un-der-stand-ing down in my heart,
4 I've got the joy,— joy,— joy,— joy— down in my heart,

Down in my heart, down in my heart! I've got the
Down in my heart, down in my heart! I've got the
Down in my heart, down in my heart! I've got the
Down in my heart, down in my heart! I've got the

Fine

joy,— joy,— joy,— joy,— down in my heart, Down in my heart to stay!
love of Je-sus, love of Je-sus down in my heart, Down in my heart to stay!
peace that pass-es un-der-stand-ing down in my heart, Down in my heart to stay!
joy,— joy,— joy,— joy,— down in my heart, Down in my heart to stay!

And it's the great-est, grand-est feel-ing, And it's a

feel-ing here to stay! And it's a joy / love / peace that needs re-

D.C.

veal-ing, So I just want to say:

Let's Pray

Lord Jesus, we know You are God. You have been with our Heavenly Father since before the beginning of time. We know You died to save us from our sins. Change our lives, Lord. We want to live for You. We ask this in Your name. Amen.

Activity Time

Add a map to the basket. Jesus said He was the Way, the Truth, and the Life. Jesus is our pathway to God. (Psalm 32:8; Isaiah 48:17; John 14:6; Hebrews 10:19–22).

Saturday/Sunday of the Second Week

Let's Pray

Dear Father God, it is with great joy we call You "Abba Father." Thank You for making us Your children. In the name of Your Son, Jesus Christ. Amen.

Reading

Galatians 4:4–7

Think about It

What does it mean to be adopted? When a child is adopted, he or she is taken into a family and is made a part of it forever. It is a binding promise that lasts for the rest of the child's life. He or she is given a special place in the family and is given a part of all the family has. An adopted child may or may not look like anyone else in the family, but he or she bears the family name.

We are adopted into God's family when we are baptized. At our Baptism, we receive a new Father, God in heaven. We receive a new family, believers in Jesus everywhere around the world. We receive a special place, an eternal home in heaven. We receive a new name, Christian. To be adopted into God's family means we are reborn and now have a life full of joy, peace, and forgiveness.

When we are baptized, we receive the gifts of forgiveness and faith. In the waters of Baptism, Jesus washes away our sins. We are forgiven through the life, death, and resurrection of our Lord and Savior, Jesus Christ. We receive faith in Jesus as our Savior through the power of the Holy Spirit. We can't come to faith on our own; only God can make us faithful.

We don't do anything when we are adopted into the family of believers; God does it all. Baptism is a binding promise. Nothing can break the promise God makes to us when we are baptized.

When the time was just right, God sent His Son to earth to make a way for us to become children of God, to be adopted into His family. God chooses to forgive us, through Jesus' work on the cross, and He chooses to bring us into His family. We are children of God forever!

What is the difference between a slave and a son? A slave lives in fear that he might displease his master. He must do everything his master says to do or he will be punished. He is not free to use anything from the household without permission. A son on the other hand, does everything he can to please his father because he loves him and he is grateful for all the father has done for him. He is not afraid of making mistakes and getting punished because he knows he will have his father's forgiveness. Everything in the household belongs to the child as well as the father.

How are people who don't believe in Jesus like slaves instead of sons? Without Jesus people can try to do many things to please God. They can try to be as good as they can, but it is not enough. The Bible says we are owned by sin. That means it is easier to sin than it is to follow God's commandments. In fact, without Jesus it is impossible to please God (Hebrews 11:6). We are trapped by our sin. And those who do not believe in Jesus will always be slaves to their sin.

But all who believe in Jesus are freed from sin and adopted as God's children (Romans 9:4). We do not obey God as a slave who is afraid of being punished, but as a son who obeys his Father with a thankful heart.

Sing!

Jesus Loves Me, This I Know

Anna B. Warner, 1820–1915

William B. Bradbury, 1816–68

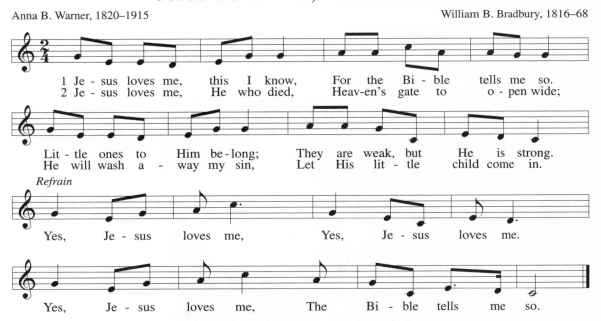

1 Je - sus loves me, this I know, For the Bi - ble tells me so.
2 Je - sus loves me, He who died, Heav-en's gate to o - pen wide;

Lit - tle ones to Him be - long; They are weak, but He is strong.
He will wash a - way my sin, Let His lit - tle child come in.

Refrain

Yes, Je - sus loves me, Yes, Je - sus loves me.

Yes, Je - sus loves me, The Bi - ble tells me so.

Let's Pray

Thank You, Jesus, for loving us and saving us. Thank You for making it possible for us to be adopted into God's family. Remind us daily of our Baptism and help us have faith and trust in You, remembering that we are children of God. In Your loving name. Amen.

Activity Time

Christians belong to God. We share God's family and God's family history. We can read all about it in the Bible (John 1:12–13; Romans 8:14–17; 1 John 3:1). Add a Bible or Bible story-book to the basket. If this basket will be a gift, take a moment to write a short note inside the front cover of the book about what Jesus means to your family.

Third Week of Lent:
Learning about What Jesus Said and Did

I am the Way
and the Truth
and the Life.
No one comes to the Father except through Me."
John 14:6

Jesus came to earth to win our salvation. He came to restore our relationship with God and to recapture the intimacy Adam and Eve had before they disobeyed in the garden. This week we will see how Jesus spent His time teaching large numbers of people and caring for the needs of individual hurting people. He is the Great Miracle Worker, Teacher, Savior, and Friend. He is the Great Seeker looking for the lost.

Materials Needed This Week

Holy Bible
Scavenger hunt lists
Whole potato

Let's Live It

1. Choose another family fast. Talk about how the first fast went and anything you would like to change this time.
2. Read one of the Gospels each evening this week. Talk about all the wonderful things Jesus did while He was here on earth.
3. Watch a Christian movie about Jesus' life. Afterward share a snack and ask each family member to tell about his or her favorite part of the movie.
4. Go to a nearby church that has "Stations of the Cross" stained glass windows. These windows show the last seven days of Jesus' life on earth before He died on the cross. Or go to an art museum in your area that has paintings of the crucifixion. Talk about what you've seen.
5. Fly kites together. After His work on earth was through, Jesus rose into heaven and returned to His Father (Acts 1:7–9). Remember that, as your kites soar toward heaven, we will one day join Jesus there.
6.
7.

Monday of the Third Week

Let's Pray

Thank You, Jesus, that we can always look to You to guide us. You are our Good Shepherd. In Your name we pray. Amen.

Reading

Matthew 9:36, 18:12–14

Think about It

Have you ever been lost? Maybe you stopped to look at a toy in a store and Mom kept going. When you looked up, she seemed to have disappeared. Or maybe you got separated from Dad in a crowd at a baseball game or amusement park.

Tell about a time when you were lost. For a moment you were surrounded by people you didn't know and who didn't know you. You didn't know where to go or who to talk to. You felt all alone. But Mom and Dad looked and looked, never stopping until you were together again. It was good to know they would come for you. That's how it is with Jesus and us.

When we sin, we are lost from God. We are so hopelessly lost that by ourselves we cannot find our way back to Him. Jesus came to earth to find us and bring us back into God's grace. *Can someone be lost and not know it?* It seems strange but the answer is yes. People who do not know Jesus as their Savior are lost and might not know it. We might think about giving up on someone who says they don't believe in Jesus. But Jesus will never give up on anyone. He loves them too much.

Today's Bible story tells about a good shepherd who cares for his sheep. A shepherd leads his sheep to good pastures to eat and drink, guides them through open land and back so they do not get lost or hurt, and protects them from predators and other dangers. The sheep can't make it on their own. Neither can we. Jesus is our Shepherd: He guides us, provides for us, and protects us. The Bible is the map our Good Shepherd gives us to make our way through life.

Will Jesus ever get tired of looking for His lost sheep? No way! Jesus loves each one of us so much that He will keep searching until He brings us home, just like a shepherd finds his lost sheep and brings them back to the flock

Sing!

I Am Jesus' Little Lamb

Henrietta L. von Hayn, 1724–82; tr. composite

WEIL ICH JESU SCHÄFLEIN BIN
Brüder Choral-Buch, 1784

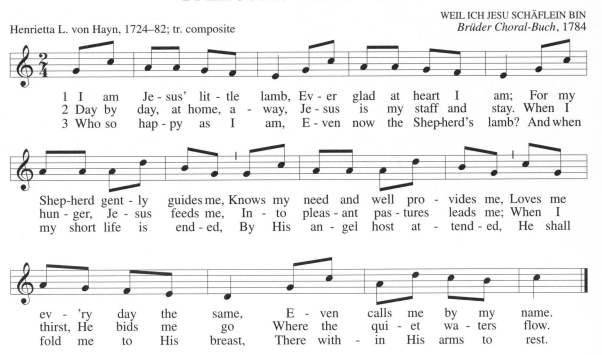

1 I am Je-sus' lit-tle lamb, Ev-er glad at heart I am; For my
2 Day by day, at home, a-way, Je-sus is my staff and stay. When I
3 Who so hap-py as I am, E-ven now the Shep-herd's lamb? And when

Shep-herd gent-ly guides me, Knows my need and well pro-vides me, Loves me
hun-ger, Je-sus feeds me, In-to pleas-ant pas-tures leads me; When I
my short life is end-ed, By His an-gel host at-tend-ed, He shall

ev-'ry day the same, E-ven calls me by my name.
thirst, He bids me go Where the qui-et wa-ters flow.
fold me to His breast, There with-in His arms to rest.

Let's Pray

Jesus, we thank You for being our Good Shepherd and for always caring for us. Keep us safe in your flock, Lord, and help us to show others the way to You. In Your holy name. Amen.

Activity Time

Play hide-and-seek with a new twist added. Choose one family member to be LOST and one family member to be the SEEKER. Send the SEEKER into another room where he cannot hear the rest of the group. Everyone else decide where the LOST one should hide, and send him there. All other family members think of one clue to give the SEEKER to help him find the LOST one. The SEEKER is then brought back into the room and told to count to 20 while everyone else hides. When the SEEKER finds any family member, they give him their clue. The game is over when the SEEKER finds the LOST one. Remember, Jesus doesn't stop looking for His lost sheep until each one is found!

Tuesday of the Third Week

Let's Pray

We praise You, Lord Jesus, that Your earthly mission has been completed, and that You never forgot why You came. You are wonderful. In Your name. Amen.

Reading

Mark 2:13–17

Think about It

Jesus came to earth with a mission. God the Father gave Him a job to do. He came to make peace between God and His children, to forgive people of their sins.

Many people reached out to Jesus. They listened to Him in huge groups in the countryside. They listened to Him at the synagogues and in the city markets. Many cried out for His healing help.

But some people wouldn't come to Jesus—sinners and tax collectors. Since they wouldn't come to Jesus, He went to them. In Jesus' time, people who followed God would avoid sinners and tax collectors. Although He was criticized for spending time with them, Jesus explained that they were part of His mission too.

In Mark 2:17, Jesus said He came to help sinners. Sinners are people who are separated from God by sin—the bad things they say, think, or do; or the good things they could have done, said, or thought, but didn't. We all are sinners. But people who are baptized and believe in Jesus as Savior are forgiven for all their sins. We are free and our friendship with God is strong.

Jesus always went to people who needed to know that God loved them so He could free them from their sin. We too can spread that Good News to others by telling them about Jesus. God helps us show His love to our friends, neighbors, and family members who don't know what Jesus does for them. We can show them by serving, giving to, and sharing with others. That is how Jesus can use us to help fulfill His mission.

How are we doing as a family sharing Jesus' love with others? What are the ways we can share the Good News of Jesus in our community? What project could we take on this Lenten season that would allow us to share Jesus?

Sing!

Have No Fear, Little Flock

Luke 12:32, st.1; Marjorie Jillson, sts. 2–4

LITTLE FLOCK
Heinz Werner Zimmermann

1 Have no fear, lit-tle flock; Have no fear, lit-tle flock,
2 Have good cheer, lit-tle flock; Have good cheer, lit-tle flock,
3 Praise the Lord high a - bove; Praise the Lord high a - bove,
4 Thank-ful hearts raise to God; Thank-ful hearts raise to God,

For the Fa - ther has cho - sen To
For the Fa - ther will keep you In
For He stoops down to heal you, Up -
For He stays close be - side you, In

give you the King - dom; Have no fear, lit - tle flock!
His love for - ev - er; Have good cheer, lit - tle flock!
lift and re - store you; Praise the Lord high a - bove!
all things works with you; Thank - ful hearts raise to God!

Let's Pray

Dear Lord God, help us to always remember that we too are sinners. Without You, we would be as lost as lost can be. Our hope and our joy and our freedom are all in You. We want to share Your love with others. Show us ways we can do that this Lenten season. In Jesus' name. Amen.

Activity Time

Prepare scavenger hunt lists for each member of your family. Put four or five common household items on each list. Some examples to include are blue thread, a penny, a safety pin, a refrigerator magnet, a washcloth, a nail, or a colored pencil. Hide each of these items in one or two rooms of your house. When everyone has found as many of the items as possible, together pray a prayer of thanks and praise that Jesus finds sinners and brings them His Good News.

Wednesday of the Third Week

Let's Pray

Dear Jesus, we are amazed at all You have done for us. We give You glory and honor. We love You, Lord. In Your name. Amen.

Reading

Matthew 22:36–40

Think about It

Jesus spent much of His time on earth teaching people God's truth. He spoke so freely and with such love that people came in large groups to hear Him (Mark 1:45). They were amazed at what He said. He forgave their sins, shared the Father's grace, and taught them to share it too. He spoke as God Himself. It seemed too good to be true. But it was true!

What did Jesus say is the greatest commandment? Jesus said the most important commandment for us to follow is to love God with all our heart, soul, and mind. To love God totally. He said the second most important commandment is to love our neighbors as ourselves.

Who are our neighbors? Are they just the families next door or are there others? In Jesus' story about the Good Samaritan, He made it very clear that our neighbor is anyone we see or meet or talk with. We are responsible for treating everyone we know with love and kindness.

Totally loving God and always being loving to others is hard to do. We can never fully keep these important commandments because we are sinful. In fact, no one has ever kept God's commandments—except one Person. Jesus is the only one who could ever obey God perfectly. Jesus paid for our sins when He died on the cross, and God forgave us. Jesus made it possible for us to freely and fully love God.

We keep the most important commandment when we worship God at church and when we rely on God to help us live out our Christian beliefs in every area of our life—at school, at work, on the ball field, playing with our friends. We show God every day that we love Him with our thoughts, attitudes, and behaviors. We keep the second most important commandment when we treat other people with love and kindness—the way we want to be treated. We give them a glimpse of God's love through our actions and attitudes.

Let's Pray

Thank You, dear Lord Jesus, that although we can never perfectly keep these two great commandments, You accept our efforts to love You and serve others in Your name. In Your holy name. Amen.

Activity Time

Play a charades game. Divide into teams or let each family member play on His own. Take turns doing charades for the following kinds of love:

How we love God: pray, go to church, read our Bible.

How we love ourselves: eat good food, wash our bodies, exercise.

How we love our neighbors: help with a chore, care for a sick neighbor, befriend a child on the playground.

54

Sing!

This Is My Commandment

John 15:11—12

Unknown

This is My com-mand-ment that you love one-an-oth-er, that your

joy may be full. full: that your joy may be

D. C, al Fine

full, that your joy may be full.

Other stanzas may be added: This is My commandment that you trust one another . . . .
serve one another . . . . .
lay down your lives . . . .

Thursday of the Third Week

Let's Pray

Jesus, You are God's holy Son. You can do great and mighty things. We worship You and give You praise for showing us how very much You love everyone. In Your loving and holy name. Amen.

Reading

John 6:1–14, 35

Think about It

Imagine this: you come to a church potluck where almost everyone forgot to bring food. The church is filled with hungry people. The pastor prays and soon there is food for everyone with more left over. Now that would be exciting! Jesus did just that in our Bible reading for today. He talked to the people gathered on a hillside, giving them spiritual food. Then, seeing their physical hunger, He gave them bread and fish too.

Why did the people gather around Jesus that day? They had seen and heard about the miracles He did for others. They too yearned for Jesus' work in their lives, to be free from sin. His words and works made them want to hear Him. His love kept them there.

Did Jesus' disciples expect this miracle? First Phillip wanted to know where all these people were going to get food. In those days, there were no restaurants nearby where they could get a quick meal. Food wasn't easy to come by. Then Andrew showed a spark of faith when he mentioned the little boy's lunch. He knew there was not enough food to go around, yet he pointed it out to Jesus.

Imagine you were one of those five thousand people. As the baskets were passed around, food was available for everyone and more was left over than the little boy brought in the first place. *What would you think about Jesus?* That He was someone special. He was not just another teacher saying good things. He was someone with power. He was the Son of God.

Sing!

Someone Special

Jaroslav J. Vajda

SOMEONE SPECIAL
Carl Schalk

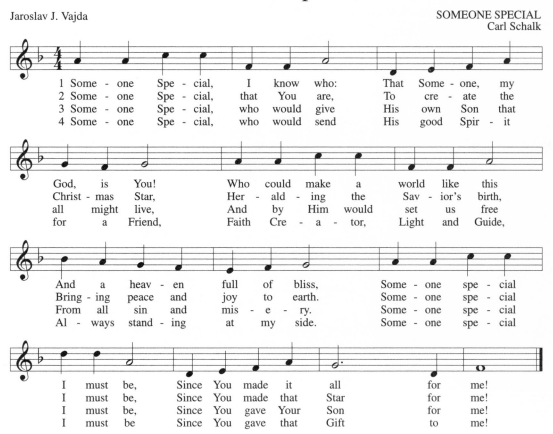

1 Some - one Spe - cial, I know who: That Some - one, my God, is You! Who could make a world like this And a heav - en full of bliss, Some - one spe - cial I must be, Since You made it all for me!

2 Some - one Spe - cial, that You are, To cre - ate the Christ - mas Star, Her - ald - ing the Sav - ior's birth, Bring - ing peace and joy to earth. Some - one spe - cial I must be, Since You made that Star for me!

3 Some - one Spe - cial, who would give His own Son that all might live, And by Him would set us free From all sin and mis - e - ry. Some - one spe - cial I must be, Since You gave Your Son for me!

4 Some - one Spe - cial, who would send His good Spir - it for a Friend, Faith Cre - a - tor, Light and Guide, Al - ways stand - ing at my side. Some - one spe - cial I must be Since You gave that Gift to me!

5 Someone Special—God and man,
You were there when I began,
You'll be there when I depart,
For You live within my heart.
Someone special—now I see,
That someone is really me.

Read John 6:35 again. Jesus calls Himself "the bread of life." What kind of bread is Jesus talking about? Just as we need to eat food to give our physical body strength, we need spiritual food from Jesus to give us spiritual strength. This spiritual food is found in the Bible, Baptism, and the Lord's Supper. When we are spiritually strong, we can please God with our thoughts, actions, and words.

Let's Pray

Thank You, Jesus, for giving up Your life on the cross, for teaching us God's Word, for being our bread of life. Help us remember that no matter what happens in our lives, we are always rich in Your love. We pray for Your sake. Amen.

Activity Time

Have everyone sit in a circle and play hot potato. Set a timer and begin passing a potato around. When the timer goes off, the one left holding the potato tells about one miracle Jesus did while He was on earth that shows He is the Son of God.

Friday of the Third Week

Let's Pray

Thank You, Lord Jesus, for this special story about Your resurrection power. We want to remember Your power and share it with the people around us who don't know Your Good News. In Your holy name. Amen.

Reading

John 11:1–6, 17–45

Think about It

The passage we just read is a very special one. It tells us a lot about who Jesus is, what He taught, and what He did. Lazarus and his sisters were close friends of Jesus. The Bible says that when Lazarus died, Jesus wept at his tomb. Jesus used this chance to show everyone His power over death.

Although the message of Lazarus's sickness got to Jesus in time for Him to reach Lazarus before he died, Jesus chose to stay where He was for two more days. *Jesus can do anything; couldn't He have kept Lazarus from dying at all?* Yes, He could have prayed and healed Lazarus immediately. But if He had done that, the people would not have seen that Jesus is stronger than death. When Lazarus died, was buried, and was then brought back to life, people knew beyond a shadow of doubt what great power Jesus had.

What did Jesus say was His reason for raising Lazarus from the dead (John 11:4; 40–41)? He wanted to bring glory to God. He knew that people would see this great miracle and be amazed by it. Jesus wanted them to see He had the power to raise them from the dead as well and to give God praise and glory.

When Jesus said, "I am the resurrection and the life," it meant that He has power over life and death. This miracle was more than the one-time event of healing Lazarus and bringing him back to life. It showed that Jesus has power over all death. Jesus' power never fails. He is able to raise up everyone who believes in Him. In that resurrection is true life with God.

Many, many people have tried to show power over death, but no one except Jesus has ever been able to do it. Jesus did it with His friend, Lazarus, and later with Himself. He promises to give us eternal life as well.

Sing!

My God Is So Great

Anonymous   Anonymous

My God is so great, so strong and so might-y! There's noth-ing my God can-not do! *(clap, clap)* The moun-tains are His, the riv-ers are His, the stars are His hand-i-work, too. My God is so great, so strong and so might-y! There's noth-ing my God can-not do! *(clap, clap)*

Let's Pray

Lord Jesus, we believe You are the Son of God. We give You glory for raising Lazarus from the dead and showing us Your resurrection power. You raised Yourself from the grave, and You will raise us from the dead and give us eternal life as well. You are wonderful. Amen.

Activity Time

Role-play the story of Jesus raising Lazarus from the dead. Let each family member choose who they want to be: Jesus, Lazarus, Martha, or Mary. Talk about what your character experienced as he or she watched this miracle happen. What did they see, think, hear, and feel?

Saturday/Sunday of the Third Week

Let's Pray

My God, You are so great, so strong, and so mighty. There really is nothing You cannot do! We are thankful that Your mighty power is at work in our lives every day. In the name of Your Son, who came to save us. Amen.

Reading

Mark 4:35–41

Think about It

Jesus and His disciples were in a small boat on the open sea in the middle of a fierce storm. The disciples were very frightened, but Jesus wasn't. In fact, He didn't even wake up!

The Bible uses the word "squall" to describe this storm. A squall is a fast-moving storm with high winds, lots of rain, and big waves. The Bible says the waves came over the sides of the boat. The boat was tossed and turned and thrown all about in the water. The disciples must have been amazed that anyone could sleep through something like that.

Jesus had no reason to be afraid. He has control over everything because He is God. His friends did not fully understand that yet. They knew He was special and had a special mission from God, but their faith in Him as the Son of God still needed to grow. The storm immediately quieted down at Jesus' demand. *What does that say about Jesus?* It shows us that He was not just a special teacher or good leader. The winds and waves obeyed Him because He created them.

Because Jesus is God, He knew ahead of time that there would be a storm. Jesus has a reason for every situation that comes into our lives. He used this storm to teach His friends about trusting in Him. He showed them they could count on His help in every situation they were in. We can count on His help too. All we need to do is call out for it. Jesus is always with us.

How did Jesus want His friends to respond to this? How does He want us to respond to His work in our lives? Jesus wanted His friends to see His great power and to feel His loving care for them. Jesus met their need. We also need to learn who Jesus is and what He does for us. We do that by reading and listening to God's Word. We can believe everything the Bible tells us. Just as Jesus calmed the storm on the Sea of Galilee, He meets our needs and helps us through all the storms of life. Whether we have problems at school or work, in our neighborhood or with our family, Jesus helps us through them.

Sing!

I Am Trusting You, Lord Jesus

Frances R. Havergal, 1836–79, alt.

STEPHANOS
Henry W. Baker, 1821–77

1 I am trust - ing You, Lord Je - sus, Trust - ing on - ly You;
2 I am trust - ing You for par - don; At Your feet I bow,
3 I am trust - ing You for cleans - ing In the crim - son flood;
4 I am trust - ing You to guide me; You a - lone shall lead,

Trust - ing You for full sal - va - tion, Free and true.
For Your grace and ten - der mer - cy Trust - ing now.
Trust - ing You to make me ho - ly By Your blood.
Ev - 'ry day and hour sup - ply - ing All my need.

5 I am trusting You for power;
   You can never fail.
   Words which You Yourself shall give me
   Must prevail.

6 I am trusting You, Lord Jesus;
   Never let me fall.
   I am trusting You forever
   And for all.

Let's Pray

You are strong and mighty, Lord Jesus! There is nothing greater than You. Help us to remember Your power and ask for Your help whenever we have a problem. Thank You for always being here. We pray in Your name. Amen.

Activity Time

Play Simon says together. Choose someone to be "Simon." Simon can ask all other members to do things like jump or crow like a rooster. If he says, "Simon says," you must do what he asks. If he doesn't, you should wait for the next command. Give everyone a chance to be Simon. Remember, God created this world by speaking the words for it to form. Jesus can control nature the same way.

Fourth Week of Lent: Giving Our Lives to Jesus

Each man should give
what he has decided
in his heart to give, not reluctantly or
under compulsion, for God loves
a cheerful giver. 2 Corinthians 9:7

What can you give to the God of the universe? What can you give to the Creator of everything? During this fourth week of Lent, we will learn that we can give something very precious back to God. We can give Him a portion of the love He has already given us. Lent is a good time to think about our friendship with Jesus and how important it is. His love is wonderful, and He makes our lives full. But it doesn't stop there. Lent is also a time when we can give love offerings back to Him: offerings of money, offerings of time spent in prayer and worship, putting Jesus first in our lives, and sharing our faith in Him with others.

Materials Needed This Week

Holy Bible
20–25 small plastic bags
Curling ribbon
Orange jelly beans
Black jelly beans
Red jelly beans
Yellow jelly beans
Purple jelly beans
Pink jelly beans
Brown jelly beans
Gray jelly beans
White jelly beans
Green jelly beans
Note cards or small sheets of paper for poem

God's Jelly Bean Rainbow

In this week's activity, we will use jelly beans to share the Good News of Jesus with others. We will put jelly beans in bags and write out a poem to go with each bag. Then we will give the bags to people to tell them about what Jesus does for us. You may decide to give them to people in a hospital, nursing home, preschool class, or Sunday school class. It is fun to share Jesus!

Here is the poem to write on note cards or sheets of paper:

Orange is the twilight night He prayed.

Black is our sin stain for which He paid.

Red is His own shed blood so bright.

Yellow is the Son's warm, healing light.

Purple is His head crowned with thorns.

Pink is hope risen on Easter morn.

Brown is the ground where He was laid.

Gray is the stone that was rolled away.

White is God's grace we freely receive.

Green our eternal life when we believe.

All of these colors represent something true:

Jesus Christ, God's own Son, died for me and died for you.

Let's Live It

Pick one or more of the activities listed below to help your family give back to God. We serve a creative God. Be creative in giving back to Him.

1. Choose a fast connected with giving. For example, parents could fast from coffee for the week and give one dollar for each cup they would have drunk to a charity. Kids could substitute their favorite drink and do the same thing.

2. During Passover, Jewish people clean out all the "leaven" from their houses. Leaven is symbolic for sin. You can clean out all the things in your house that are still useful but that you don't need anymore. Donate them to a charity.

3. Buy movie tickets and an ice cream gift certificate. Give them to a family who is struggling financially.

4. Have a "secret angel" week. Put the names of all your family members in a bowl. Everyone draw out one name. Secretly do special things for that person all week. It might be doing their chores, buying them a favorite candy bar, or letting them go first when it is really your turn. Make their life special this week. On Saturday, have everyone reveal whose "angel" they were.

5. Start a batch of friendship bread (suggested recipe follows). When it is ready, give some to a friend. When we share love, we never run out. There is always more to give.

6.

7.

Friendship Bread Starter

1 pkg. active dry yeast	2 c. sugar
2 1/2 c. warm water	1 tbsp. sugar
4 c. flour	2 c. milk

Note: Do not use metal utensils or bowls! Metal will react with the ingredients.

Day one: Dissolve yeast in 1 cup of warm water. Stir in the rest of the water, 2 cups of flour, 1 tablespoon of sugar, and mix well. Cover with plastic wrap and set on counter. (Don't put it in the refrigerator.)

Day two: Stir.

Day three: Stir.

Day four: Stir.

Day five: Add 1 cup sugar, 1 cup flour, 1 cup milk, and mix well.

Day six: Stir.

Day seven: Stir.

Day eight: Stir.

Day nine: Do nothing.

Day ten: Add 1 cup sugar, 1 cup flour, 1 cup milk, and mix well.

Divide starter into four equal parts. Put three parts in zipper plastic bags to give to friends along with directions to make their own bread. This will be their "day one."

To your leftover starter add:

1 c. oil	3 eggs
1 c. sugar	1 large box of vanilla pudding
2 c. flour	2 tsp. cinnamon
1 1/2 tsp. baking powder	1/2 tsp. salt
	1 c. raisins or nuts

Mix well. Heat oven to 325 degrees. Bake for one hour or until knife stuck in the middle comes out clean. (Adapted from Amish Friendship Bread Starter, Lancaster.about.com/library/specials/blrec8.htm)

Monday of the Fourth Week

Let's Pray

Dear Lord God, we are so thankful for all You do for us. Help us to be cheerful givers in everything we do. In Jesus' name. Amen.

Reading

Luke 21:1–4 and 2 Corinthians 9:7

Think about It

This Bible story tells us about rich people who gave generous offerings to their church. It also tells us that a very poor woman also gave her offering, but it was much less than what the others gave. Jesus noticed the widow's giving, but He didn't look at the amount. Jesus looked in her heart, at her motive—why she did it. He looked at what it cost her to give.

What was special about the widow's gift? She gave because she loved God. She didn't give from the extra money she had, she gave all of her money. That's the same way Jesus gives to us. When He died on the cross, He gave us everything.

What attitude does God want us to have when we give? The Bible tells us that God loves a cheerful giver; someone who gives because he or she wants to and not because they have to. You may have heard some people say this kind of giving is from the heart. It doesn't matter what the gift is—money, doing a chore without being asked, or a birthday present to a friend. When we do it with love and not out of obligation, our giving is pleasing to Jesus.

Our motive for giving is much more important to Jesus than the actual value of what we give. As God's children, we can give freely to others from the love He first gives us. God's love is too wonderful to keep to ourselves, so we want to share it. This kind of sharing is one way we show how thankful we are to Him.

Do you have to wait until you are grown up to share Jesus' love with others? Never think that you can't do much for Jesus because you are young. He knows how you feel inside about

Him. That love turns even the smallest activity into the greatest gift, just like the widow's small coins pleased Jesus more than the many coins from the rich man. When you do something kind for someone else, it is a great gift in Jesus' eyes.

Sing

Take My Life, O Lord, Renew

Frances R. Havergal, 1836–79, alt.

PATMOS
William H. Havergal, 1793–1870

1 Take my life, O Lord, re-new, Con-se-crate my heart to You;
2 Take my hands and let them do Works that show my love for You;
3 Take my voice and let me sing Prais-es to my Sav-ior King;
4 Take my love; my Lord, I pour At Your feet its treas-ure store;

Take my mo-ments and my days; Let them sing Your cease-less praise.
Take my feet and lead their way, Nev-er let them go a-stray.
Take my lips and keep them true, Filled with mes-sag-es from You.
Take my self, Lord, let me be Yours a-lone e-ter-nal-ly.

Let's Pray

Lord God, You are such a giving God. Help us share the love You give so freely with others around us. Give us eyes that see the needs around us and hearts to meet those needs. In the name of Jesus, the greatest gift You gave us. Amen.

Activity Time

Set up the plastic bags and put an orange, black, and red jelly bean in each bag. Orange helps us remember Jesus' night of prayer at Gethsemane. Black reminds us of the sin we were trapped in. Red represents Jesus' blood that set us free.

Tuesday of the Fourth Week

Let's Pray

Dear Jesus, we want to be like Mary and sit at Your feet. Help us to learn from Your Word, the Bible, so we can live lives that are pleasing to You. In Your name. Amen.

Reading

Luke 10:38–42

Think about It

Do you like to listen to a good story? To sit and hear a storyteller weave a tale, draw you in, and excite you? That's how Mary felt as she sat at Jesus' feet. Jesus was so interesting! His words made Mary feel happy. They helped her know how to obey and please God. Jesus' teaching gave Mary hope and comfort. She didn't want to miss a single word, so she sat near Him and listened.

Her sister, Martha, was worried about how to take care of all the people who came to hear Jesus. Who would feed them? Where would everyone sit? Where would they sleep? Martha was worried about all the work she had to do. She was upset with Mary for not helping her.

Martha wanted Jesus to do something about it. And He did. *But did Jesus do what Martha expected?* Instead of scolding Mary and telling her to get to work, Jesus praised her for wanting to learn about His mission. He also reminded Martha that although caring for guests is important, spending time with God is the most important thing we can do.

Martha was very worried by all the things she had to do to be a good hostess. *Is that wrong?* She wanted to take care of everyone who came to hear Jesus talk. But it was a lot of work to make a big meal all by herself. She knew many of the people would even be spending the night at her house and would need places to sleep. Martha was so concerned about everything around her that she forgot to listen to Jesus. She forgot that His story was the reason everyone was coming in the first place.

Do you ever get so involved in things around you that you forget to listen to Jesus? It happens to all of us. Sometimes we have to stop doing things—even good and necessary things—so we can listen to Jesus. Try to listen to Him every day by reading His stories in the Bible and by listening to your parents and to your Sunday school teachers and pastor. It is important to spend time with Jesus each day so we can serve Him in all that we do.

Sing!

Jesus Loves Me, This I Know

Anna B. Warner, 1820–1915

William B. Bradbury, 1816–68

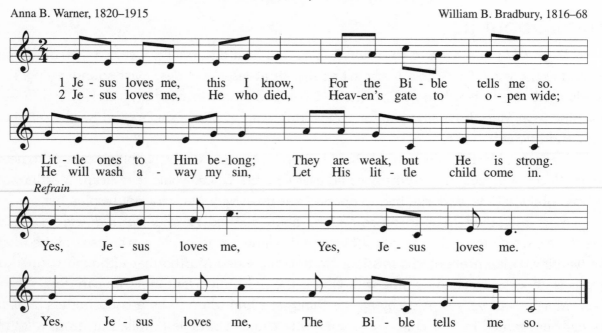

Let's Pray

Jesus, You speak words of truth, words that make our lives better. We want to listen to everything You say. Help us to have ears to hear You, like Mary. And help us to serve You, like Martha. We ask this for Your sake. Amen.

Activity Time

Put a yellow, purple, and pink jelly bean in each bag. The yellow jelly bean reminds us of Jesus' light that shows us the way to God. The purple one is a reminder of His kingly authority that was mocked with the crown of thorns. When we see the pink jelly bean, we think about the hope that became ours on Easter morning.

Wednesday of the Fourth Week

Let's Pray

Jesus, as we gather now to look at Your Word, help us understand what it means in our lives. In Your name. Amen.

Reading

Luke 18:18–30

Think about It

The young man, a leader in his community, tried very hard on his own to gain new life with God so he would go to heaven someday. Yet he was afraid he was not doing enough, so he asked Jesus, "How can I get to heaven?" Jesus' answer surprised him very much. Jesus told him that it is not what you do that gets you into heaven—it's who you love.

How had the young man tried to get into heaven? He tried to follow God's laws, the Ten Commandments. When Jesus listed the laws—do not murder, do not steal, honor your parents—the young man honestly said he had tried his best to keep these laws. Yet he knew he was still missing something. That is what brought him to Jesus.

We know from the other Gospel accounts of this conversation that this young man probably became an important leader. He had many material things and those things were very important to him. But he was missing one important thing—Jesus. Jesus wanted the young man to love Him with all his heart. One way for the young man to show this love was to share his wealth—to give his possessions away. This was hard because his riches were more important to him than Jesus.

Does that mean we have to give away all our money, toys, and clothes before we can go to heaven? No. Jesus does not command us to give away our possessions. He commands us to love Him. The young man in this story loved his things more than Jesus. When our earthly things start taking our love away from Jesus, we need to choose: follow our wants or follow our Lord.

What gets in your way of loving God? Can you think of something in your life that is taking your love away from Jesus? It could be anything that keeps you from obeying God's Word and living it out in your life.

How do we receive eternal life in heaven with Jesus? Read John 3:15, Acts 16:31, and Ephesians 2:8–9. Eternal life in heaven is a gift that Jesus has already given us. We need only to believe in Jesus, the Son of God. He died on the cross to take away our sins. He rose again and is sitting at the right hand of God, the Father. Only Jesus gives us eternal life in heaven.

Sing!

In You Is Gladness

Johann Lindemann, 1549–1631
Tr. Catherine Winkworth, 1829–78, alt.

IN DIR IST FREUDE
Giovanni Giacomo Gastoldi, c. 1556–1622

1 In You is glad - ness A - mid all sad - ness, Je - sus
2 If He is ours, ... We fear no pow - ers, Not of

sun - shine of my heart. By You are giv - en The gifts of
earth or sin or death. He sees and bless - es In worst dis -

heav - en, You the true Re - deem - er are. Our souls are
tress - es; He can change them with a breath. Where - fore the

wak - ing, Our bonds are break - ing, Who trusts You sure - ly Has built se -
sto - ry Tell of His glo - ry With hearts and voic - es; All heav'n re -

cure - ly And stands for - ev - er. Al - le - lu - ia! Our hearts are
joic - es In Him for - ev - er. Al - le - lu - ia! We shout for

pin - ing To see Your shin - ing, Dy - ing or liv - ing To You are
glad - ness, Win o - ver sad - ness, Love Him and praise Him And still shall

cleav - ing Now and for - ev - er. Al - le - lu - ia!
raise Him Glad hymns for - ev - er. Al - le - lu - ia!

Let's Pray

Jesus, You are the holy Son of God. You are our Lord. Help us to put You first in our lives. Show us areas that take more of our attention and love than they should. Yes, we believe in You, Jesus. Amen.

Activity Time

Add the brown, gray, white, and green jelly beans to the bags. The brown helps us remember Jesus really died and the gray that He was buried. The white jelly bean is a reminder of God's grace which we receive through Jesus' death. The green reminds us of our eternal life in heaven.

Thursday of the Fourth Week

Let's Pray

Thank You, Lord God, for leaving us Your Word. We believe everything You say in the Bible and we believe in Jesus as our Savior. We praise You for Your greatness. In Your Son's name. Amen.

Reading

Matthew 8:5–13

Think about It

The man in this Bible story is an excellent example of faith. The centurion, a Roman soldier, had a lot of responsibility and authority. People immediately obeyed his commands. When his servant became ill, he knew Jesus could help. Although he could have, the centurion did not order Jesus to come to his house or demand that He heal the servant. Instead, the soldier believed in who Jesus was and in His power to heal. He said he knew that all Jesus had to do was say the word and the servant would be healed. Jesus was pleased with this soldier's faith. He healed the servant immediately and told His followers that people with faith like the centurion's would go to heaven.

How do we know the soldier had faith? He showed faith by recognizing Jesus' power and authority. He knew Jesus' power was greater than any sickness. His faith was key to the servant being healed.

What is so important about having faith? Faith in Jesus saves us from our sin and makes God and His love real to us. *How do we get faith?* Faith comes from God. We cannot make it happen on our own. Instead, the Holy Spirit gives us faith through Baptism and God's Word. True faith is believing that Jesus died on the cross for us. When we have faith, we believe what the Bible says about God, our heart is filled with love for Him, and we want to worship Him, obey His Word, and serve Him in every way we can.

How can we show faith like the Roman soldier? We can know for certain that Jesus is God. He is our heavenly King and has power over everything on this earth—even sin. When we believe Jesus as Savior and trust in His love, knowing that He always answers our prayers, we show this kind of faith.

Let's Pray

Lord Jesus, help us to believe in You with faith like the centurion's. Help us remember all You have done for us and all You continue to do for us and for other people through us. Help us to be faithful to You. We pray this in Your name. Amen.

Sing!

My Faith Looks Trustingly

Ray Palmer, 1808–87

OLIVET
Lowell Mason, 1702–1872

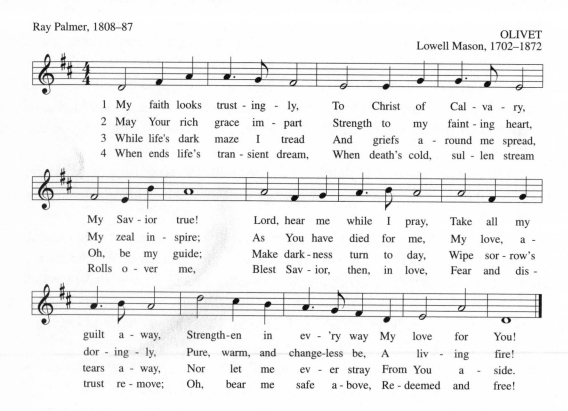

1 My faith looks trust-ing-ly, To Christ of Cal-va-ry,
2 May Your rich grace im-part Strength to my faint-ing heart,
3 While life's dark maze I tread And griefs a-round me spread,
4 When ends life's tran-sient dream, When death's cold, sul-len stream

My Sav-ior true! Lord, hear me while I pray, Take all my
My zeal in-spire; As You have died for me, My love, a-
Oh, be my guide; Make dark-ness turn to day, Wipe sor-row's
Rolls o-ver me, Blest Sav-ior, then, in love, Fear and dis-

guilt a-way, Strength-en in ev-'ry way My love for You!
dor-ing-ly, Pure, warm, and change-less be, A liv-ing fire!
tears a-way, Nor let me ev-er stray From You a-side.
trust re-move; Oh, bear me safe a-bove, Re-deemed and free!

Activity Time

Write out the poem, "God's Jelly Bean Rainbow," found on page 66. Tape or staple it to the bags and add a bow made from the curling ribbon. Give the bags to people with whom you want to share the Gospel.

Friday of the Fourth Week

Let's Pray

Thank You, Jesus, for making a clear path for us to follow. Although it is not always easy for us, You always light the way. Amen.

Reading

Matthew 4:18–22, 6:19–24

Think about It

Have you heard anyone say, "When I grow up I'm always going to do what I want to"? Children have a lot of people in their lives who tell them what to do—parents, teachers, aunts and uncles, brothers and sisters, babysitters. Sometimes it seems like adults can do whatever they feel like. But adults know that is not true. As we see in today's Bible reading, everyone must make some important choices about what to do.

The first verses tell about Jesus calling the first disciples. He asked them to stop the kind of work they were doing and begin a different kind of work—spreading the Gospel message of Jesus. The disciples left the work their families asked them to do and followed a different path. Everyone chooses a path in life. In fact, this is a choice we ask God to help us make every day: to follow Jesus and give our lives to Him.

Today's Bible reading is also about deciding what to value. In these verses, Jesus talks about choosing to value our possessions or our relationship with God. Jesus said wherever we put our treasures—how we spend our effort and time—is where our heart will be. Jesus' friends loved Him and His commands more than they loved being fishermen, so they went with Him when He asked them to. When we listen to and obey God's Word, we show that we love Jesus. Jesus wants us to use our talents and abilities to bring glory to God and serve Him.

What did Jesus mean that our "eye is the lamp of the body"? How can our eye be bad (Matthew 6:22–23)? Jesus is not talking about our physical eye but what we look at with our eyes that can be good or hurtful. For example, if we choose to spend a lot of time watching TV shows that teach us to be sassy with our parents, selfish with our toys, or hurtful to others, our eyes are letting the "darkness" of sin hurt us. The TV shows we watch, the books we read, or the video games we play can bring either more of God's light into our life or more of sin's darkness.

Can we do what the world says to do and do what God says to do? No. If we want to follow Jesus, we can't serve ourselves and ignore what God tells us in His Word, the Bible. When we follow Jesus, we listen to His Word and obey it even when it is not easy to do. Everyone follows something. Jesus' way is always right. It will always lead us on the path toward heaven.

Sing!

This Little Gospel Light of Mine

Traditional — Traditional

1 This lit-tle Gos - pel light of mine, I'm going to let it shine;
2 All a - round the neigh-bor-hood I'm going to let it shine;
3 Hide it un - der a bush-el? No! I'm going to let it shine;

This lit-tle Gos - pel light of mine, I'm going to let it shine;
All a - round the neigh-bor-hood I'm going to let it shine;
Hide it un - der a bush-el? No! I'm going to let it shine;

This lit-tle Gos - pel light of mine, I'm going to let it shine,
All a - round the neigh-bor-hood I'm going to let it shine,
Hide it un - der a bush-el? No! I'm going to let it shine,

Let it shine all the time, Let it shine.
Let it shine all the time, Let it shine.
Let it shine all the time, Let it shine.

Let's Pray

Lord Jesus, help us to follow You and to store up treasures in heaven. We want to serve You. Give us ideas from Your Word, and also as we go about our lives, about how to be better followers of You. We ask these things in Your loving name. Amen.

Activity Time

Continue to copy the poem "God's Jelly Bean Rainbow." Attach it to the remaining bags and close them with the curling ribbon. Pray for the people who will receive the bags.

Saturday/Sunday of the Fourth Week

Let's Pray

Lord Jesus, You are our Lord and our God. We believe in You as our Savior. You died on the cross for our sins. We believe You are alive today and with us wherever we are. Amen.

Reading

John 3:16, 20:24–31

Think about It

Believing is the key to following Jesus: Believing that Jesus is the Son of God, died on the cross for our sake, rose from the dead, and lives in heaven with God, the Father, and in our hearts.

Jesus' Word is true, yet sometimes we doubt. We wonder. Thomas, one of Jesus' close friends wondered too. Thomas was there with Jesus, he actually heard all the things Jesus said and saw all the things Jesus did. But he still wondered if it all was really true.

Was Jesus angry with Thomas for doubting? Jesus loved Thomas and He came to show him that everything since His crucifixion had happened just the way the other disciples said. Jesus wants to show us He is true too. He does that through the Bible, through pastors, through other people who love Him, and through His Holy Spirit who helps us believe. He is not angry when we have questions. Jesus wants to answer our questions with His truth.

What did Thomas do when he saw the wounds on Jesus' hands? Immediately Thomas cried out, "My Lord and my God!" His heart jumped for joy. Jesus was alive, and everything He taught about God and eternal life was true! Thomas believed. We can have that same joy when we believe Jesus is our Savior who was sent from God, died on the cross, and rose again from the grave.

According to verse 31, why was this Gospel written? It was written so we may believe that Jesus is the Christ, the Son of God, and that by believing we may have life in His name. It was written so we could become Christians too.

Thomas needed to see physical evidence before he would truly believe. *What does Jesus say about those of us who haven't seen Him face-to-face and still believe?* In verse 29 He says those who haven't seen but believe in Him anyway are blessed. Faith is when we believe what God teaches in the Bible without actually seeing it. Hebrews 11:6 says that without faith, it is impossible to please God. So when we say with Thomas, "My Lord and my God," our words 'aith are pleasing to our Father in heaven.

1

Sing!

Praise Him, Praise Him

Anonymous, c. 1890

Carey Bonner, 1859–1938

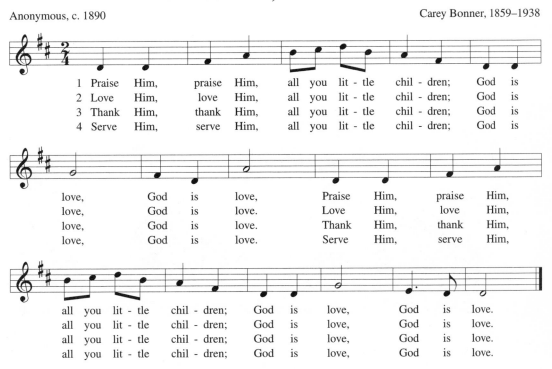

1 Praise Him, praise Him, all you lit - tle chil - dren; God is
2 Love Him, love Him, all you lit - tle chil - dren; God is
3 Thank Him, thank Him, all you lit - tle chil - dren; God is
4 Serve Him, serve Him, all you lit - tle chil - dren; God is

love, God is love, Praise Him, praise Him,
love, God is love. Love Him, love Him,
love, God is love. Thank Him, thank Him,
love, God is love. Serve Him, serve Him,

all you lit - tle chil - dren; God is love, God is love.
all you lit - tle chil - dren; God is love, God is love.
all you lit - tle chil - dren; God is love, God is love.
all you lit - tle chil - dren; God is love, God is love.

Let's Pray

Lord Jesus, forgive us for our sins and help us to be faithful followers of Your Word.
When we sometimes doubt or wonder, help us believe Your Word. Amen.

Activity Time

Deliver your jelly bean bags. Pray again for the people who receive them that Je
will warm their hearts.

"Love the Lord your God with all your heart and with all your soul and with all your mind. This is the first and greatest commandment."
Matthew 22:37—38

Once we believe in who Jesus is and what He has done for us, the Holy Spirit fills our hearts with the desire to respond. God gave His Word so we would know what He wants us to do. The fruit of our faith through obedience is our love gift to Him. We respond to God's love with our service, generosity, and willingness to share all the blessings God has given to us (1 Timothy 6:17–18). It is through living out our faith that we can truly have the full and abundant life Jesus promised us.

Materials Needed This Week

Holy Bible
Small pad of notepaper
Pieces of curling ribbon to tie notepaper
Pencils
Medium-sized basket

This week your family will have the chance to think about and recognize all the ways you respond to Jesus and obey Him. Each evening after your devotion, think about the ways you have been obedient and write them on notepaper. You will read them together at the end of the week.

Let's Live It

1. Choose a fast to do either as a family or as individuals. Remember that fasting is an act of worship to our living God.

2. Catch 'em in the Act. Be on the lookout for family members showing the fruit of the Spirit in their lives. Make a fruit of the Spirit tree to keep track of the harvest. At the end of the week, celebrate with a special treat and rejoice at how Jesus is at work in your lives.

3. Play Simon says. Remind your children that Jesus loves to see His children obey His Word.

4. Go on a treasure hunt around your home to find things that have to be connected to other things in order to work. These things might be electrical devices that must be plugged in, table legs that have to be connected to the table to hold it up, or pictures that to have a nail to stay hooked on the wall. It is important to stay connected to Jesus.

5. Dress up in first-century clothing and eat a simple meal: fish, nuts, fruit, and pita bread. Sit on the floor and eat with your hands. A lot has changed in the world since Jesus walked among us as a man, but one thing has stayed the same: He loves us with an everlasting love.

6.

7.

Monday of the Fifth Week

Let's Pray

Thank You, Lord Jesus for Your great love. It is so wonderful to be loved by You. Help us to share Your love with everyone we meet. We pray in Your name. Amen.

Reading

John 15:9–17

Think about It

Jesus knew He would go back to heaven. He talked with His friends, the disciples, about how they should live when He was no longer with them in person. This message is for us too. The Bible tells us that loving Jesus and His Father in heaven and loving one another are the most important things we can do. God's love will help us love other people. Jesus also promised to give us joy as we stay close to Him. We feel this joy when we love other people. It's Jesus' love flowing out of us to them.

How did Jesus show His love to us and His obedience to His heavenly Father? Jesus obeyed His heavenly Father at a great price. When He came to earth to die for our sins, He put His Father's will and our need above Himself. We have peace with God because Jesus was obedient even to death on the cross. He received the punishment; we received the peace and grace. How can we not love and obey Him after all that!

Can anyone love us more than Jesus? Jesus Himself said, "Greater love has no one than this, that he lay down his life for his friends" (John 15:13). There are stories of parents, spouses, or even friends dying to save a loved one, but only Jesus laid down His life so completely for so many. There is no one like Him.

How can we have His joy and peace? We can have a joyful and satisfying life by trusting in His love for us and living as God's children, obeying all that He teaches us in His Word. Jesus said, "If you keep My commands, you will remain in My love, just as I have obeyed My Father's commands and remain in His love" (John 15:10).

Will our obedience get us to heaven? No! Eternal life is God's gift to us by His grace when we believe Jesus died for our sins. Nothing we do can get us into heaven. Living out our faith through obedience brings us joy because it gives us an opportunity to show Jesus how much we love Him.

What is the greatest commandment? "Love the Lord your God with all your heart and with all your soul and with all your mind" (Matthew 22:37). The second greatest commandment follows it: "Love one another that they may see your good deeds and praise your Father in heaven" (Matthew 5:16). Be as kind and as forgiving and as loving to one another as Jesus is to us. Don't let even one day go by without shining the light of Jesus' love to someone else.

Sing!

I've Got the Joy

Traditional   Traditional

1 I've got the joy,— joy,— joy,— joy— down in my heart,
2 I've got the love of Je - sus, love of Je - sus down in my heart,
3 I've got the peace that pass - es un - der - stand - ing down in my heart,
4 I've got the joy,— joy,— joy,— joy— down in my heart,

Down in my heart, down in my heart! I've got the
Down in my heart, down in my heart! I've got the
Down in my heart, down in my heart! I've got the
Down in my heart, down in my heart! I've got the

Fine

joy,— joy,— joy,— joy,— down in my heart, Down in my heart to stay!
love of Je - sus, love of Je - sus down in my heart, Down in my heart to stay!
peace that pass - es un - der-stand-ing down in my heart, Down in my heart to stay!
joy,— joy,— joy,— joy,— down in my heart, Down in my heart to stay!

And it's the great - est, grand - est feel - ing, And it's a

feel - ing here to stay! And it's a joy / peace love that needs re -

D.C.

veal - ing, So I just want to say:

Let's Pray

Dear Jesus, thank You for laying down Your life for us. We know that it is only by Your grace that we are saved. It is by nothing we have done on our own. Help us to pass that kind of love to the other people in our lives today and every day. Amen.

Activity Time

Take a minute to think of ways you were obedient to Jesus today. Write each one on a separate sheet of notepaper. Roll it up like a scroll, tie it with a piece of curling ribbon, and put it in your basket.

Tuesday of the Fifth Week

Let's Pray

Thank You, Jesus, for setting us free from sin and its control in our lives. Help us to serve You in everything we do. Thank You for loving us each day. Amen.

Reading

John 8:31–36

Think about It

Being a Christian is a long-term relationship. Our friendship with Jesus lasts a lifetime. But like any friendship, spending time together makes it stronger. In today's passage, Jesus says that when we hold to His teaching, we grow stronger in faith. In other words, we stay close with Jesus by reading His Word; listening to our pastors, teachers, and parents; and praying. Jesus forgives our sins and sets us free. He helps us live lives that are pleasing to God the Father.

How can we know we are really Jesus' disciples (friends)? Jesus makes it simple. Those who believe in Him, day after day, are His disciples. If we believe, then we know we are His disciples. As disciples, we want to know God's Word and live it. When we sin, we confess and ask for Jesus' help to keep us from committing the same sin again. Sometimes following Jesus is called "a walk." As we go through life, we are taking a walk with Jesus. He's been down this path Himself and made a safe way for us to go.

What do His disciples know? What is the truth? We know that Jesus is the Son of God. He came to earth to die on the cross and save us from our sins. We know that He rose from the dead and is alive today. His Spirit lives within the hearts of all who believe. This is the truth that brings us salvation and eternal life in heaven.

What are we set free from? We are set free from the power of our sin and the punishment of hell. Jesus' death on the cross not only paid our punishment, but it took away sin's power to control our lives. We are now controlled by the power of God. We can't break the power of sin by ourselves, but Jesus can. In fact, He has already broken sin's power by taking our sins to the cross. All we need to do is believe, confess our sins, and ask for His help!

Each of us must choose who our master will be, God or sin. Jesus offers a life of freedom for us. Sin offers a life of pain. Remember, we know we are His disciples when we believe and follow His teaching. Show Him your friendship by living a life of faith and obeying His Word today.

Let's Pray

Help us, dear Lord God, to keep learning from You and Your Holy Word every day. Help us stay close to You and follow what You say. In Jesus' name. Amen.

Activity Time

Think of ways you lived out your faith in Jesus today. Write each one on a separate sheet of notepaper. Roll it up like a scroll, tie it with ribbon, and put it in your basket.

Sing!

Amazing Grace

NEW BRITAIN

John Newton, 1725–1807, alt.

J. Carrell and D. Clayton, *Virginia Harmony*, 1831

1 A - maz - ing grace! How sweet the sound That
2 The Lord has prom - ised good to me, That His
3 Through man - y dan - gers, toils, and snares I
4 Yes, when this flesh and heart shall fail And

saved a wretch like me! I once was lost but
word my hope se - cures; He will my shield and
have al - read - y come; His grace has brought me
mor - tal life shall cease, A - maz - ing grace shall

now am found, Was blind but now I see!
por - tion be As long as life en - dures.
safe so far, His grace will see me home.
then pre - vail In heav - en's joy and peace.

91

Wednesday of the Fifth Week

Let's Pray

Dear God, You are the Giver of life. We need You to live and grow, like a plant needs the sunshine and rain to live and grow. Thank You for caring for us. In Jesus' name we pray. Amen.

Reading

John 15:1–6 and Galatians 5:22–23

Think about It

Have you ever heard of an apple growing without a tree or a watermelon growing without a vine? Fruit can't grow unless it is connected to a plant. The same thing is true for us. We can't grow as Christians unless we are connected to Jesus. He is our vine, giving us His love, His Word, and His guidance through the Holy Spirit. He helps us grow spiritually.

We grow the "fruit of the Spirit" but we don't grow into apples, watermelons, or strawberries. When we abide in Christ, the fruit of the Spirit grows in our lives. He helps us become more and more like Him.

Fruit needs the vine or tree to get nutrients and energy from the sunshine, soil, and water. It is impossible to grow fruit without the vine or tree to support it. In the same way, it is impossible to follow Jesus and be His disciple without spending time with Him, reading, and learning His Word. We need Jesus to survive as much as we need food to survive. He teaches us how to love Him and obey Him. We can best learn how to love others when we have been loved by Jesus Himself.

Galatians 5:22 lists nine character traits that are called the fruit of the Spirit: love, joy, peace, patience, kindness, goodness, faithfulness, gentleness, and self-control. *What fruit is in your life? What spiritual fruit do you see in one another's lives?* Encourage one another as you see spiritual fruit growing.

Sing!

What a Friend We Have in Jesus

Joseph Scriven, 1820–86

CONVERSE
Charles C. Converse, 1832–1918

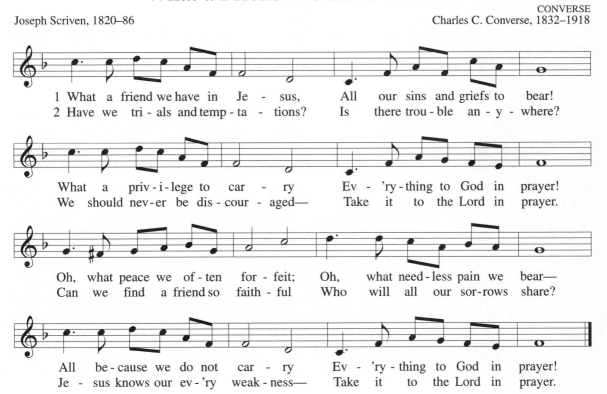

1 What a friend we have in Je - sus, All our sins and griefs to bear!
2 Have we tri - als and temp - ta - tions? Is there trou - ble an - y - where?

What a priv - i - lege to car - ry Ev - 'ry - thing to God in prayer!
We should nev - er be dis - cour - aged— Take it to the Lord in prayer.

Oh, what peace we of - ten for - feit; Oh, what need - less pain we bear—
Can we find a friend so faith - ful Who will all our sor - rows share?

All be - cause we do not car - ry Ev - 'ry - thing to God in prayer!
Je - sus knows our ev - 'ry weak - ness— Take it to the Lord in prayer.

Let's Pray

Thank You, Jesus, for being our vine, for giving us new life. May we always desire to abide in You. Help us to continue to grow and bear spiritual fruit so we are more like You. Help us live so You are glorified. In Your name we pray. Amen.

Activity Time

Take a minute to think of ways a family member showed the fruit of the Spirit in their life today. Write each one on a separate sheet of notepaper. Roll it up like a scroll, tie it with ribbon, and put it in your basket.

Thursday of the Fifth Week

Let's Pray

We praise You, Jesus, for all You have done for us. You made the great sacrifice by coming to earth and dying on the cross. Help us know how to share Your love with others. Amen.

Reading

Matthew 16:24–28

Think about It

Following Jesus is not always easy. Jesus said we have our own cross to carry when we are His followers. Following Him affects our whole lives. It is not something we decide to do for one day and then go off in another direction the next. It is a long journey that we take one step at a time every day of our lives.

Today, not many of us expect to sacrifice our lives for the Gospel, but what are some other things we might have to give up to abide with Jesus? We may have to give up watching certain TV programs or movies because they do not honor God. We may not be able to be on a sports team that plays games on Sunday mornings. We may have to get up a little early to have time to read God's Word. The things we sacrifice are different. The reason is the same. Anything that gets in our way of following Jesus has to go.

Sometimes the thought of giving up something is hard. We like having it in our life and we want to keep doing it, although it may not be the best for us. That's when it is good to remember what Jesus did for us. He left heaven and became both God and man. He chose to not use His spiritual powers to make His life on earth easy. He chose to go through the false trial, the beatings, and death because He loves us and wants us to spend eternity in heaven with Him. When we think of that, it is easier to make changes in our own lives.

Why do sacrifices have to be made at all? Wouldn't it be nice to be in a world where no one had to sacrifice, where everything was filled with love and life was easy? Unfortunately, we live in a sin-filled world. That is why Jesus had to come in the first place. God's enemy, Satan, works very hard to spread sin and the pain that comes with it. Today's passage asks what good is it to have a fun-filled life on earth—doing and having everything you want—if you lose eternal life?

Is there anything the Holy Spirit has brought to mind during this devotion that might be keeping you from following Jesus? Bring it to Jesus in prayer and ask for His help in giving it up.

Sing!

Glory Be to Jesus

Italian, 18th cent.
Tr. Edward Caswall, 1814–78

WEM IN LEIDENSTAGEN
Friedrich Filitz, 1804–76

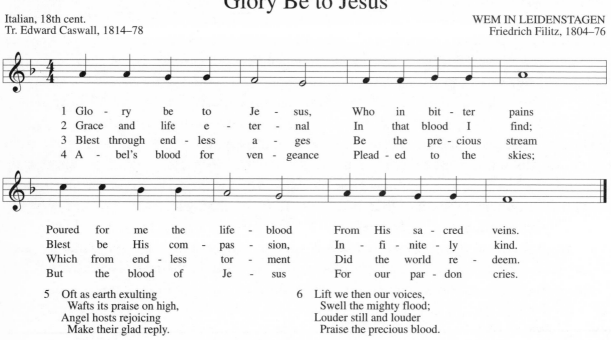

1 Glo - ry be to Je - sus, Who in bit - ter pains
2 Grace and life e - ter - nal In that blood I find;
3 Blest through end - less a - ges Be the pre - cious stream
4 A - bel's blood for ven - geance Plead - ed to the skies;

Poured for me the life - blood From His sa - cred veins.
Blest be His com - pas - sion, In - fi - nite - ly kind.
Which from end - less tor - ment Did the world re - deem.
But the blood of Je - sus For our par - don cries.

5 Oft as earth exulting
   Wafts its praise on high,
   Angel hosts rejoicing
   Make their glad reply.

6 Lift we then our voices,
   Swell the mighty flood;
   Louder still and louder
   Praise the precious blood.

Let's Pray

Thank You, Jesus, for Your great sacrifice for us. Anything we do ourselves is so small compared to it. Help us remember that through the Holy Spirit, we find new life in You. We pray in Your name. Amen.

Activity Time

Take a minute to think of ways you saw other family members living out their faith and being obedient to Jesus today. Write each one on a separate sheet of notepaper. Roll it up like a scroll, tie it with a piece of ribbon, and put it in your basket.

Friday of the Fifth Week

Let's Pray

We praise You, Jesus, for always reaching out to us, guiding us, and protecting us so we can be obedient to Your calling in our lives. Amen.

Reading

Luke 5:1–11

Think about It

Jesus didn't sit and wait for people to come to Him for salvation and friendship. He went out to them. Today's passage tells us that He was teaching a big group of people near the Lake of Gennesaret. At the same time, He was reaching out to one particular fisherman named Simon Peter. Peter was just coming into port from a long night of working. He was tired and wet and weary, and he didn't find any fish. But in obedience to Jesus, he stopped to let down his nets one more time.

Peter was ready to believe and quick to obey when Jesus gave him the command. We can do that too. As we go about our normal activities, we can listen for the Holy Spirit's voice telling us what to do or say.

What did Jesus ask Peter to do? Jesus asked him to throw out his fishing nets one more time. We do not know whether Peter really thought he would catch more fish, but we do know he trusted Jesus. *What did Peter discover after he obeyed Jesus?* Peter discovered who Jesus really was, God's Son, and he saw his own sinfulness. As we learn more and more about who Jesus is, we clearly see our own sinfulness and are reminded of our need for forgiveness through Jesus as Savior. He is holy, all knowing, all wise. He is God. Knowing Jesus reminds us who we are—God's own, adopted children.

In the Bible reading for today, Jesus gave Peter a new job. He made Peter a "fisher of men." That means He called Peter to lead people to God by telling them about Jesus. In later years, Peter told many about forgiveness, love, and eternal life through Jesus, our Savior.

Jesus moved Peter to action. *Can you think of a time when God's Word moved you to action?* Share a time when you put in practice a lesson from Sunday school, a sermon, or a devotion you read. Just like Peter, you listened to Jesus' words and went to work.

Sing!

Go, My Children, with My Blessing

Jaroslav J. Vajda

AR HYD Y NOS
Welsh melody, 18th cent.

1 Go, My chil-dren, with My bless-ing, nev-er a-lone.
2 Go, My chil-dren, sins for-giv-en, At peace and pure.
3 Go, My chil-dren, fed and nour-ished, Clos-er to Me;
4 I the Lord will bless and keep you And give you peace.

Wak-ing, sleep-ing, I am with you; You are My own.
Here you learned how much I love you, What I can cure.
Grow in love and love by serv-ing, Joy-ful and free.
I the Lord will smile up-on you And give you peace:

In My love's bap-tis-mal riv-er I have made you Mine for-ev-er.
Here you heard My dear Son's sto-ry; Here you touched Him, saw His glo-ry.
Here My Spir-it's pow-er filled you; Here His ten-der com-fort stilled you.
I the Lord will be your Fa-ther, Sav-ior, Com-fort-er, and Broth-er.

Go, My chil-dren, with My bless-ing— You are My own.
Go, My chil-dren, sins for-giv-en, At peace and pure.
Go, My chil-dren, fed and nour-ished, Joy-ful and free.
Go, My chil-dren; I will keep you And give you peace.

Let's Pray

Dear Jesus, when we ask You to forgive our sins and be our Savior, we know You already did so when You died on the cross for us. We know You are walking right beside us, guiding us in everything You want us to do, because You said so in the Bible. Help us to share that Good News by being good fishers of men. Amen.

Activity Time

Take a minute to think of ways you saw other family members living out their faith and being obedient to Jesus today. Write each one on a separate sheet of notepaper. Roll it up like a scroll, tie it with ribbon, and put it in your basket.

Saturday/Sunday of the Fifth Week

Let's Pray

Dear God, we praise You for the courage You give us to live Christian lives in front of our friends and neighbors. Thank You for the Good News of salvation to share. For Jesus' sake. Amen.

Reading

Matthew 28:16–20

Think about It

When Jesus returned to heaven, He gave the disciples an important job. Each generation of believers since then has worked very hard at this same job. In fact, we are all still working at it. Jesus told us to go throughout the world and tell people about Him so they could receive eternal life too. This job is called the Great Commission.

When Jesus gave us this job, He made us His ambassadors. That means we tell people who Jesus is and how they can meet Him. We show them who Jesus is by living out His commands in our everyday lives. What Jesus does for us is too wonderful to keep to ourselves. Let's share it with everyone!

Ever since Jesus gave this command, He has continued to help His followers obey it. But the world is a big place, and new people are born every day. Each and every one of these people need Jesus. Some believers faithfully tell their own friends and family members right here at home. Others go to faraway countries to share the Gospel. Together we can all do our part for this mission.

The Bible tells us over and over that Christians are children of God. We are part of God's family. Even our name, Christian, shows who we stand for. Believing in Jesus and helping people go hand in hand. We share God's love by bringing others food, clothing, and sometimes building shelters. We share the truth of the Bible with them, telling them what Jesus has done and how much He loves them.

What are some specific ways we can live out the Great Commission? We can tell the people right in our neighborhood and school who don't know Jesus who He is and what He does for them. We can also give money to missionaries who tell people about Jesus. We can pray regularly for missionaries and for friends and family members who don't know Jesus' love. We can share food and clothing or help build homes and shelters. Watch for a need someone might have and ask God to help you do your part to meet it.

Jesus promised to always be with us (Matthew 18:19–20). He is right beside us, helping us every step of the way as we live out the Great Commission. His Spirit lives in our hearts, guiding us and giving us the strength we need to do His will.

Let's Pray

Dear Jesus, guide us in sharing Your truth with the people around us. Use our words and lives to show people Your love for them. We pray for the missionaries You send to other nations. Speak Your truth through them. Show us ways we can help them and remind them that You are always with us. In Your loving name. Amen.

Sing!

He's Got the Whole World in His Hands

IN HIS HANDS
American spiritual

American spiritual

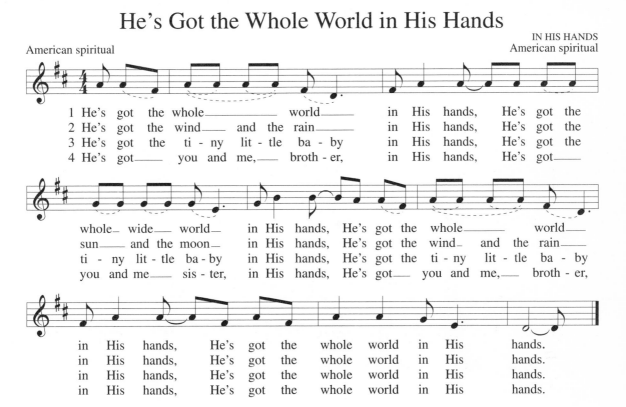

1 He's got the whole_____ world_____ in His hands, He's got the
2 He's got the wind____ and the rain_____ in His hands, He's got the
3 He's got the ti - ny lit - tle ba - by in His hands, He's got the
4 He's got_____ you and me,____ broth - er, in His hands, He's got_____

whole_ wide____ world__ in His hands, He's got the whole_____ world____
sun____ and the moon___ in His hands, He's got the wind_ and the rain_____
ti - ny lit - tle ba - by in His hands, He's got the ti - ny lit - tle ba - by
you and me____ sis - ter, in His hands, He's got____ you and me,____ broth - er,

in His hands, He's got the whole world in His hands.
in His hands, He's got the whole world in His hands.
in His hands, He's got the whole world in His hands.
in His hands, He's got the whole world in His hands.

Activity Time

One by one, open the scrolls you have placed in the basket this week. Take turns reading all the ways your family has been obedient to God. Spend time as a family praising God and giving Him thanks for working in your lives. Thank Him for allowing you to be His children and for showing you how to serve Him in all you do.

Sixth Week of Lent:
Serving Jesus in Our Family and Community

"And the second is like it:
Love your neighbor as yourself."
Matthew 22:39

Through faith, we are firmly connected to Jesus. Cleansed with His forgiveness, healed by His mighty power, and abiding in His love, He enables us to carry His message to the hurting world that needs Him so desperately. This week we will think about how and where we can serve our Lord, giving back to Him out of the abundant life He has given to us.

Materials Needed This Week

Holy Bible

    This week's activity section is different from the others in this book. This time your family will decide upon a way to put your faith into action. Choose an act of service you can do as a family. It might be something at your church or your school or somewhere else within your community where you know there is a need. Use daily activity times to plan and carry out your service. On the last night, discuss together how it all went.

Let's Live It

    There are many things we can do to serve our Savior. As a family, we can sponsor a needy child, volunteer at a food bank or homeless shelter, or visit a nursing home or hospital and share the Good News of Jesus Christ.

1.   Choose a fast connected to serving. Perhaps you can fast from a regular family activity and instead pack care boxes at a local food bank or visit residents of a nursing home.

2.   Find a service project for your family to do, such as collect all the food needed to prepare an Easter dinner and give it to a needy family.

3.   Help serve a meal at a homeless shelter.

4.   Appoint a "servant" at each evening meal this week. This person will bring needed things to the table during the meal and will clean up the table afterward. Remind your children that even Jesus washed His disciples' feet.

5.   Volunteer to do a project at church or school, such as pick up all the litter on the school grounds, complete a painting project, or clean the bathrooms.

6.   Find a neighbor or older person from your church who needs something done around their house and, as a family, do it for them.

7.

Monday of the Sixth Week

Let's Pray

Dear Lord Jesus, Your idea of a good leader is so different from what the world says a good leader is. Help us always to remember that our actions please You best when we put others first. Teach us to be leaders by serving others in Your name. Amen.

Reading

Mark 10:35–45

Think about It

"I get to be first!" "I want to be leader!" We all like being first. We like getting the best seat to watch TV or sitting by the window in the car. Jesus' friends, the disciples, were no different than we are. Two of them, James and John, even asked Jesus to save the best spots in heaven for them.

Jesus must have really surprised them when He said the best spots in heaven don't go to the people "in charge"—the leaders, but to those who serve. This is a hard idea to understand. We usually think leaders are the ones who get rewarded. Yet Jesus teaches that those who are great in His kingdom are those who serve others out of love for God. They do everyday chores without complaining. They do what needs to be done without expecting recognition, praise, or anything in return.

Jesus said the greatest leaders are servants, not rulers over others. Godly servants lead by showing love to people around them and meeting their needs, whatever those needs may be. They think of other people before they think of themselves.

How do godly servants put the needs of others ahead of themselves? If someone needs food, they get it for them. If they need clothes, they find some for them. If Mom needs help with the dishes or dinner, a servant does it cheerfully. If a teacher needs help passing out papers, a servant volunteers. If someone drops all their books, a servant helps pick them up. When a godly servant helps meet a need, God's love is poured out through them and everyone feels its warmth.

Jesus is the greatest example of a godly servant. Jesus did what He taught others to do—He put our needs before His own. He left His heavenly home with all of its glory and humbled Himself by becoming our servant. Jesus died an awful, painful death on the cross so we can have God's love, forgiveness, and eternal life (Philippians 2:6–8).

Think of someone you know who is a servant-leader, someone who tries to follow Jesus' example and puts the needs of others first. Maybe it's your mom or dad. Parents work very hard to provide food, clothes, a home, and many other things for their children. Maybe it's your child. She or he follows Jesus and shows others His love by cheerfully doing the things they are asked to do. Maybe it's the lunch lady who faithfully serves good food each day with a smile. Maybe it's your pastor or a missionary you know. Jesus' love shines through His servants, whatever the task they are doing.

Let's Pray

Dear Lord Jesus, help us to be faithful servants for You. We don't want praise or glory; we want only to show our gratitude to You. Help us see opportunities to serve You in our home and in our neighborhood. Call on us; we want to serve You! We ask this in Your holy name. Amen.

Activity Time

Think of any needs you know about at your church, school, and community. These might be personal needs of a family or a ministry at church, like the food bank. Maybe your school grounds need some litter picked up. Maybe your family could visit church members in a nursing home. Maybe a family with a new baby would appreciate a ready-made meal delivered to their door. Brainstorm together about how you can serve God in a special way this week. Pray and ask God to show you which need He wants you to meet.

Sing!

This Little Gospel Light of Mine

Traditional   Traditional

1 This lit-tle Gos - pel light of mine, I'm going to let it shine;
2 All a - round the neigh-bor-hood I'm going to let it shine;
3 Hide it un - der a bush-el? No! I'm going to let it shine;

This lit - tle Gos - pel light of mine, I'm going to let it shine;
All a - round the neigh-bor-hood I'm going to let it shine;
Hide it un - der a bush - el? No! I'm going to let it shine;

This lit - tle Gos - pel light of mine, I'm going to let it shine,
All a - round the neigh-bor-hood I'm going to let it shine,
Hide it un - der a bush - el? No! I'm going to let it shine,

Let it shine all the time, Let it shine.
Let it shine all the time, Let it shine.
Let it shine all the time, Let it shine.

Tuesday of the Sixth Week

Let's Pray

Praise You, Lord Jesus, giver of all that is good and holy. You make us able to do the work You have set before us. We pray in Your name. Amen.

Reading

Matthew 25:14–30

Think about It

One way Jesus taught people was by telling them stories. These stories are called parables. In the parable we read today, Jesus said that a master gave his three servants talents, or money. He didn't ask the servants to make more money for him; he only wanted them to be faithful with what he gave.

Was the master fair in what he asked the servants to do? Verse 15 says the master gave to each according to his own ability. He trusted each servant to work as hard as he could, to do his best with what he had. The servants weren't to compare themselves with anyone else. They were to be faithful with the talents their master gave them.

Was the master pleased when he returned? He was very pleased with the first two servants. They did just what he asked. He was pleased that his trust in them was repaid in a job well done, and he joyfully rewarded them. The third servant betrayed his master's trust when he did not even try to please his master. He turned out to be someone who was not very trustworthy.

Does doing your best mean being perfect? No; only Jesus is perfect. All He asks from us is that we rely on Him to help us do our best and try our hardest in whatever task is ahead of us. When we face a big job, like a test at school, Jesus doesn't expect us to have a perfect score. He does want us to try our hardest to answer as many questions as we can correctly. When we do that, we can rejoice even before we know our grade because we did what Jesus asked.

What talents has Jesus given to you? How are you using them? The Bible says each of us is fearfully and wonderfully made (Psalm 139:14). God has created us to be just who He wants us to be. We each have talents and spiritual gifts that make me, me and make you, you (Romans 12:6; James 1:17). No two people have the same gifts and talents. Our God is a wonderfully creative God, He never runs out of new combinations!

Sing!

Take My Life, O Lord, Renew

Frances R. Havergal, 1836–79, alt.

PATMOS
William H. Havergal, 1793–1870

1 Take my life, O Lord, re - new, Con - se - crate my heart to You;
2 Take my hands and let them do Works that show my love for You;
3 Take my voice and let me sing Prais - es to my Sav - ior King;
4 Take my love; my Lord, I pour At Your feet its treas - ure store;

Take my mo - ments and my days; Let them sing Your cease - less praise.
Take my feet and lead their way, Nev - er let them go a - stray.
Take my lips and keep them true, Filled with mes - sag - es from You.
Take my self, Lord, let me be Yours a - lone e - ter - nal - ly.

Let's Pray

Lord Jesus, help us to be faithful servants. We know that You are always right here to help us serve. Thank You for being a faithful and trusting master. Help us praise You by working hard at whatever task we have. Amen.

Activity Time

Continue doing the act of service your family decided to do on Monday of this week.

Wednesday of the Sixth Week

Let's Pray

We praise You, heavenly Father, for Your quiet work in this world, for touching each of us. Your love is always here and we are thankful for it. In Your Son's loving name. Amen.

Reading

Matthew 6:1–6, 16–18

Think about It

Today's Scripture is very clear. If we brag about what we do for God and want people to notice how much we are serving the Lord, then our only reward is our own bragging. It's okay for people to praise you for a job well done, but if that is your main reason for doing it, you are serving man not God.

On the other hand, when we quietly pray, fast, and help others out of love and care for them, we are serving Jesus. It is a heart issue. It's your motive, the reason behind doing what you are doing. Everyone needs encouragement and praise, and Jesus puts people into our lives to do just that. It feels wonderful to be praised for a job well done. It is like frosting on a cake, beautiful to look at and sweet to eat. Serving to please Jesus is like the cake. It's the reason there is frosting. When you serve Jesus with a loving heart and still happen to get praised, then it's as if you have your cake and eat it too.

What does verse three mean when it says do not let your left hand know what your right hand is doing? This is a figure of speech, a way of saying don't call attention to yourself when you are giving or serving. *How many times has someone in our church stood up and announced, "I am giving $1,000 to Jesus today"?* We would probably be shocked if someone did that. Instead, each person is to quietly give their offerings and pass the basket along.

Who sees every act of love and service we do, big or small? Jesus. He doesn't miss even the smallest act of kindness. He is with us every minute of every day. When He sees us obeying His commands, sharing His love, and serving others in His name, our acts of kindness please Him. Do your good deeds quietly, but remember that your Savior sees each act of kindness.

If you have fasted this Lenten season, was it hard not tell others what you were doing? How did you handle it? It can be hard to be quiet about a sacrifice, especially if it is a big one for you. We are excited about following Jesus and want others to know. Sometimes we need encouragement from the people around us when we try something new. *How did you cope with that?* Don't worry if you think you weren't quiet enough—Jesus knows your heart. He loves you!

Sing!

My Faith Looks Trustingly

Ray Palmer, 1808–87

OLIVET
Lowell Mason, 1702–1872

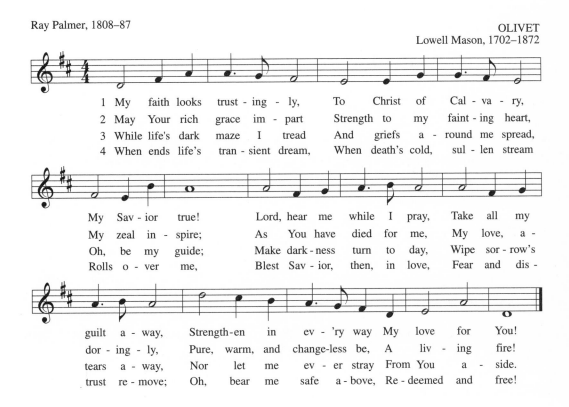

1 My faith looks trust - ing - ly, To Christ of Cal - va - ry,
2 May Your rich grace im - part Strength to my faint - ing heart,
3 While life's dark maze I tread And griefs a - round me spread,
4 When ends life's tran - sient dream, When death's cold, sul - len stream

My Sav - ior true! Lord, hear me while I pray, Take all my
My zeal in - spire; As You have died for me, My love, a -
Oh, be my guide; Make dark - ness turn to day, Wipe sor - row's
Rolls o - ver me, Blest Sav - ior, then, in love, Fear and dis -

guilt a - way, Strength-en in ev - 'ry way My love for You!
dor - ing - ly, Pure, warm, and change-less be, A liv - ing fire!
tears a - way, Nor let me ev - er stray From You a - side.
trust re - move; Oh, bear me safe a - bove, Re - deemed and free!

Let's Pray

Dear God, be our encourager as we seek to serve You. Guide us to do the things You want us to do. Receive our gifts, our prayers, and fasting as acts of worship that we give to You in love. Continue to teach us Your perfect way. In Jesus' name. Amen.

Activity Time

Continue your act of service.

Thursday of the Sixth Week

Let's Pray

Jesus, we praise You and give You glory. You are the Wonderful Counselor, Mighty God, Eternal Father, Prince of Peace. You are the greatest Giver and the greatest Gift ever given. Amen.

Reading

Matthew 25:34–46

Think about It

Throughout His earthly ministry, Jesus cared for hurting people. He showed them God's love in many ways. He met their physical needs and their spiritual needs. He helps us to do the same. Whether we bring a meal to a family with a new baby, give an older person a ride to church, or visit someone in the hospital, we are sharing Jesus' love as we help people.

Does Jesus know we are serving Him? Jesus sees and knows everything because He is God. In the Bible, He tells us how to serve, and He gives us the Holy Spirit who helps us know when there is a need we can help with.

What kinds of ways does this passage say we should help people? Jesus is talking about practical ways to serve others. We can meet their physical needs with food, clothes, care, and companionship. Sometimes, even before hurting people can really believe Jesus loves them, acts of kindness can help them feel His love.

How does your family do that? We don't have to go far to find people with needs. They are all around us in our churches, schools, and neighborhoods. Most churches have programs to help those in need. Workers are always welcome at food banks, clothing distribution centers, and homeless shelters. Lonely people in hospitals and nursing homes are always happy to receive friendly cards or short visits. We can donate our extra clothes and toys to organizations that give them to needy people. We can also give money to Christian organizations that help needy children all over the world.

Beyond everything else, we can pray for service groups, missionaries, and Christian leaders who give their lives to bring hope to the hurting.

Who did Jesus say the righteous are really feeding and clothing and visiting? They are helping Jesus. *Why would He say that?* Jesus loves every person on earth, and whenever we do acts of kindness in His name, we are doing it for Him. Each kind act shows our love for Jesus and shares His love with someone in need. Jesus sees and remembers every act of kindness.

Let's Pray

Lord Jesus, You are a great giver. Help us to grow to be more and more like You. Give us eyes and ears that recognize the needs You want us to meet. Helps us share Your love with everyone! Amen.

Activity Time

Continue your act of service.

Sing!

Jesus Loves Me, This I Know

Anna B. Warner, 1820–1915

William B. Bradbury, 1816–68

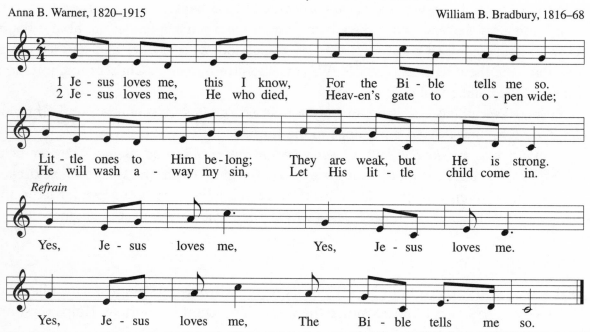

1 Je - sus loves me, this I know, For the Bi - ble tells me so.
2 Je - sus loves me, He who died, Heav-en's gate to o - pen wide;

Lit - tle ones to Him be - long; They are weak, but He is strong.
He will wash a - way my sin, Let His lit - tle child come in.

Refrain

Yes, Je - sus loves me, Yes, Je - sus loves me.

Yes, Je - sus loves me, The Bi - ble tells me so.

114

Friday of the Sixth Week

Let's Pray

Lord Jesus, thank You for the mercy and grace You show us. Thank You for the peace and love we have each day because of Your mercy. You are awesome. Amen.

Reading

Luke 6:27–35 and Galatians 6:10

Think about It

Love your enemies. This is very hard. Surely Jesus didn't mean you should love the boy who pushed you, the classmate who teased you, or the teacher who marked up your paper after you worked so hard on it. Hang on to your hat because those are the very people Jesus did mean!

It is easy to love people who love us back. But it is nothing special to love and serve those who love us anyway. Even people who don't have faith in Jesus do that. Loving those who are unkind or unfair is part of being a Christian. How Christians treat their enemies shows God's love at work.

What does it mean to "love your enemies"? We are to treat them with the same love and kindness we would give to our friends. Christians are called to be like Christ. Jesus showed mercy to us and He wants us to treat others the way He treats us. Although we will still make mistakes, Jesus helps us try. Christians are called to show God's wonderful and mighty love to the world, love that can bring healing and peace and hope to their lives. We are showing them that God's love is greater than human love.

What is mercy? Mercy is showing forgiveness and kindness when it is undeserved. Revenge is man's way. Mercy is God's way. We can leave all our hurt and anger in God's hands, knowing that Jesus died for us and loves us even when we sin. He will help us turn in love to the person who hurt us.

Is there someone in your life who has hurt you or repaid your kindness with hate? Talk about those painful experiences, then take a moment to pray for the people involved. Ask God to help you be merciful. We can love and forgive those who hurt us because we have received Jesus' love and forgiveness in our lives.

Sing!

God Loves Me Dearly

August Rische 19th cent.
Tr. composite

GOTT IST DIE LIEBE
German folk tune

1 God loves me dear - ly, Grants me sal -
2 I was in slav - 'ry, Sin, death, and
3 He sent forth Je - sus, My dear Re -
4 Je - sus, my Sav - ior, Him - self did

va - tion, God loves me dear - ly, Loves e - ven me.
dark - ness; God's love was work - ing To make me free.
deem - er, He sent forth Je - sus And set me free.
of - fer; Je - sus, my Sav - ior, Paid all I owed.

Refrain

There - fore I'll say a - gain: God loves me

dear - ly, God loves me dear - ly, Loves e - ven me.

5 Now I will praise You,
   O Love Eternal;
   Now I will praise You
   All my life long. *Refrain*

Let's Pray

Sometimes it is hard to follow Your teachings, Lord Jesus. Loving our enemies isn't easy. Forgive us when we want to lash out at them. Remind us of Your mercy, and help us be merciful to them. We pray this for Your sake. Amen.

Activity Time

Continue your act of service with your family.

Saturday of the Sixth Week

Let's Pray

We praise You, Lord God, for the opportunity to be workers in Your church. Help us plant and water the seeds of Your truth. In Jesus' name. Amen.

Reading

1 Corinthians 3:5–9

Think about It

Sometimes it's hard to understand the spiritual truths taught in the Bible. That's why word pictures are often used. In this Bible passage, the apostle Paul uses the word picture of planting a seed and watering it to help new believers understand how important it is to tell others about Jesus.

117

When we tell others about Jesus and how He saved us, we plant the seeds of knowledge about God's love for the world through Jesus. When we show Christian love and kindness, the seeds are watered. *Planting seeds and watering them is very important work, but can we actually make a seed grow?* No. Just like it is only God who can make the flowers we plant and water grow, so it is only God who makes faith grow.

Will everyone who hears about Jesus or sees acts of Christian kindness believe right away? We can never know the answer to that because God alone creates faith in every believer's heart. But we do know that God uses our words and our faith-filled actions to plant the seeds and water them.

What seeds are we planting and watering? We are planting words from the Bible, God's truth. We water these seeds with the fruit of God's Spirit—love, joy, peace, patience, kindness, goodness, faithfulness, gentleness, and self-control. And we trust God the Holy Spirit to make them grow.

Let's Pray

Dear Lord Jesus, help us not to become discouraged as we plant and water seeds for Your harvest. Give us many chances to serve You each day. In Your name we pray. Amen.

Activity Time

How did your service project go? Did you do what you set out to do or did your project change as the week went on? If you try another family project, what would you do differently? Describe how this experience helped your family grow closer. Thank God for His help in your project and ask for more project ideas.

Sing!

This Little Gospel Light of Mine

Traditional   Traditional

1 This lit-tle Gos - pel   light of mine,   I'm going to let it   shine;
2 All   a - round___the   neigh-bor-hood   I'm going to let it   shine;
3 Hide it___ un - der a   bush-el? No!   I'm going to let it   shine;

This   lit - tle Gos - pel   light of mine,   I'm going to let it   shine;
All   a - round___ the   neigh-bor-hood   I'm going to let it   shine;
Hide   it___ un - der a   bush-el? No!   I'm going to let it   shine;

This   lit - tle Gos - pel   light of mine,   I'm going to let   it   shine,
All   a - round___ the   neigh-bor-hood   I'm going to let   it   shine,
Hide   it___ un - der a   bush - el? No!   I'm going to let   it   shine,

Let   it   shine   all   the   time,   Let   it   shine.
Let   it   shine   all   the   time,   Let   it   shine.
Let   it   shine   all   the   time,   Let   it   shine.

119

Palm Sunday: Receiving Jesus as Our King

Blessed is He who comes in the name of the Lord!
Mark 11:9b

Let's Pray

Dear Lord Jesus, prepare our hearts each day to welcome You as our King. We praise You, Son of God, for all You have done for us. Amen.

Reading

Matthew 21:1–11

Think about It

Often in His ministry, Jesus quietly slipped in and out of towns, going about His business. Yet on this day, He rode into Jerusalem for everyone to see. He came in like a king riding on a donkey. In those days, when a king rode a donkey, it meant he came in peace instead of war. The Bible says Jesus is the Prince of Peace. He came to give each of us God's peace and love (John 14:27). He knew what was going to happen to Him on the cross later that week, but He came anyway because He wanted the people to know how much He loved them.

What did Jesus show everyone by riding into Jerusalem on a donkey? He showed them He was their King; and like a good king, He wanted to bring His people hope, peace, and love. God sent Jesus on a mission. That mission was to forgive our sins and to help us be at peace with God. When we believe in Jesus and trust in Him, our sins are forgiven. We can have peace, love, and joy no matter what happens in our lives.

The crowds of people were happy and excited about Jesus. They were saying, "Yes, You are our Lord, we believe in You! We want God's peace and forgiveness." They showed their love for Him by laying down their coats and palm branches for Him to ride over. It was like rolling out the red carpet to show Jesus honor and respect—unlike later in the week when He would be treated horribly.

How do we show Jesus today that we love Him? We can show Jesus that we love Him in many different ways: by spending time with Him in prayer and in worship at church, by listening to our pastors, parents, and teachers talk about Jesus, and by reading the Bible and doing what it says. Jesus said, "If you love Me, you will obey what I command" (John 14:15, 21, 23).

What are some ways our family can show our love by serving Him? In the Bible, Jesus tells us a great way to show Him our love is to love other people as much as we love ourselves (Matthew 22:38). *Is there a neighbor who needs to feel Jesus' love through us?* Could we mow their lawn, bake a batch of cookies, help baby-sit their small children, pray for them? How can we let Jesus' love shine through our lives?

Sing!

In You Is Gladness

Johann Lindemann, 1549–1631
Tr. Catherine Winkworth, 1829–78, alt.

IN DIR IST FREUDE
Giovanni Giacomo Gastoldi, c. 1556–1622

1 In You is gladness Amid all sadness, Jesus sunshine of my heart. By You are given The gifts of heaven, You the true Redeemer are. Our souls are waking, Our bonds are breaking, Who trusts You surely Has built securely And stands forever. Alleluia! Our hearts are pining To see Your shining, Dying or living To You are cleaving Now and forever. Alleluia!

2 If He is ours, We fear no powers, Not of earth or sin or death. He sees and blesses In worst distresses; He can change them with a breath. Wherefore the story Tell of His glory With hearts and voices; All heav'n rejoices In Him forever. Alleluia! We shout for gladness, Win over sadness, Love Him and praise Him And still shall raise Him Glad hymns forever. Alleluia!

Let's Pray

Lord Jesus, we too sing out, "Hosanna to the Son of David!" just like the people of Jerusalem. Blessed are You! Thank You for being our Heavenly King, our Prince of Peace. Amen.

Activity Time

Role-play Jesus' ride into Jerusalem. Pick a donkey (someone with a strong back). Let the smallest child play the role of Jesus. Everyone else can be the townspeople. Lay your coats on the floor and call out, "Hosanna, hosanna in the highest!" as Jesus rides by. We can still rejoice because Jesus is our King!

Holy Week: Remembering Jesus' Last Week

...by His wounds we are healed. Isaiah 53:5b

During this week before Easter, we will remember in our devotions the great joys and sorrows that Jesus and His followers experienced. Use it as an opportunity to discuss these powerful emotions with your family. Talk about the awful effects of sin in your own lives and upon Jesus in His sacrifice for everyone. Know the joy of His love in that He did all of this for you. Take that love and hope and share it with friends, neighbors, and family members who don't know His love.

Materials Needed This Week

Holy Bible

Have the following colored eggs ready: white, black, orange, green, purple, and gold

Basket for the eggs

Let's Live It

1. Make "Resurrection Cookies" before Easter morning (suggested recipe follows).

2. Get a lamb cake mold and have fun baking and decorating your own Easter lamb.

3. Go to church on Good Friday and afterward talk with your family about how Jesus' sacrifice has affected your lives. Try to spend the rest of the evening as quietly as possible without TV, video games, or computers. Think about His love for you.

4. Greet this wonderful Easter Day at dawn. Go to a sunrise service.

5. Celebrate Easter Sunday. Wear your finest clothes. Have egg hunts. Jesus has risen and we are His children. Experience the joy!

6.

7.

Resurrection Cookies

1 c. pecans
1 t. vinegar
Pinch of baking soda
1 recloseable plastic bag
3 egg whites
1 c. sugar
Rolling pin
Masking tape

1. Preheat oven to 325 degrees. Put pecans into plastic bag and have children use the rolling pin to break them into pieces. Set aside. *"Jesus was wounded for us."* Beat egg whites until stiff peaks form. *"Jesus' body was broken for us."* As you are beating, add the sugar a little at a time. *"Jesus loves us with an everlasting love."*

2. Let each child smell the sour vinegar. *"Jesus was offered vinegar to drink on the cross."* Add it to the egg whites. Next add the baking soda. *"God's resurrection power would bring Jesus back from the dead."* Gently fold in the pecans and drop by teaspoons onto a cookie sheet you have lined with wax paper.

3. Turn **off** oven and put cookies in. Tape the door shut with the masking tape. *"Soldiers sealed the stone in front of His tomb."* Go to bed. In the morning, take the cookies out of the oven let everyone try them. They are hollow on the inside, just like the tomb on Easter morning. *"He has risen! He had risen indeed!"*

Monday of Holy Week

Let's Pray

Thank You, dear Savior, for giving us Your Word to help us remember what happened in Your life right before the crucifixion. We are thankful that Your Word and what it tells us about Your sacrifice for us is true. In Your holy name. Amen.

Reading

Matthew 26:17–32

Think about It

(Although the events we are reading about now took place on a Thursday, we are talking about them early so we can spend more time this week looking closely at what happened later that night after the Last Supper in the Upper Room.)

Jesus and His friends were in Jerusalem to celebrate a Jewish holiday called Passover. Jesus took this time to tell His followers about the changes He knew were coming. He used every chance to teach them, encourage them, and prepare them for living lives that were godly and pleasing to Him. He wanted to help them get ready for what was going to happen. And He wanted to give them a new celebration to remember the lasting sacrifice He was making.

What is Passover? Passover is when Jewish people celebrate the night God freed the Hebrews from slavery in Egypt. You can read about it in Exodus 1–15. On that night, Hebrew families were told to kill a lamb and wipe its blood on the lintel and posts of the door, showing that inside the house was a family who loved God. The angel of death passed over every house that was marked this way. He didn't punish them for their wrongdoing; He passed over their sin. Jewish people today still eat a Passover meal and remember God's miracles that night.

What does the blood of the lamb have to do with Jesus' death? The Bible calls Jesus the Lamb of God (John 1:29; 1 Peter 1:19; Isaiah 53:7). Jesus is the Lamb that takes away, or covers, our sin. In the same way the blood of the Passover lamb covered the Hebrews' sin, Jesus stood in our place and took the punishment for all of our sins. The best news is that the covering of Jesus' blood lasts forever. It never has to be done over.

The Passover meal Jesus ate with His disciples is called the Last Supper. *Do you know of anything we do at church that reminds us of this Last Supper?* Jesus started a new tradition for His followers during this Passover meal. He instituted, or started, the Lord's Supper, which we also call Holy Communion. While Christians no longer eat a full Passover meal together, we do take the bread and drink the wine to remember Jesus' sacrifice for our sins. Holy Communion is one way believers see and taste God's grace for us. It is something Christians have done and will continue to do until Jesus comes back.

What is Holy Communion? Jesus broke the bread, handed it to His friends, and told them it was His body broken, just like the Passover lamb, for them (and for us). Then He gave them the cup of wine and told them it was His blood of a new covenant with them. It was His blood shed for the forgiveness of their sins (and ours) with the promise, or covenant, that this forgiveness is forever. Just like the blood from the Passover lamb covered the household and showed their relationship with God, Jesus' blood shows that our sins are forgiven and that God has shown us His love through Christ.

Let's Pray

Thank You, Jesus, for rescuing us from a life of slavery to sin. Thank You for being our Passover Lamb. Help us to remember that although Your forgiveness is free to us, it came at a great price to You! Amen.

Sing!

Glory Be to Jesus

Italian, 18th cent.
Tr. Edward Caswall, 1814–78

WEM IN LEIDENSTAGEN
Friedrich Filitz, 1804–76

1 Glo - ry be to Je - sus, Who in bit - ter pains
2 Grace and life e - ter - nal In that blood I find;
3 Blest through end - less a - ges Be the pre - cious stream
4 A - bel's blood for ven - geance Plead - ed to the skies;

Poured for me the life - blood From His sa - cred veins.
Blest be His com - pas - sion, In - fi - nite - ly kind.
Which from end - less tor - ment Did the world re - deem.
But the blood of Je - sus For our par - don cries.

5 Oft as earth exulting
   Wafts its praise on high,
  Angel hosts rejoicing
   Make their glad reply.

6 Lift we then our voices,
   Swell the mighty flood;
  Louder still and louder
   Praise the precious blood.

Activity Time

Place a white egg in your Easter basket. White stands for our pure, clean Passover Lamb—Jesus Christ.

Tuesday of Holy Week

Let's Pray

We praise You, Jesus, for Your faithfulness to Your disciples and to us. We thank You that You didn't change Your mind about dying for us even when You suffered. Help us to stand true to You and Your Word when we are faced with difficulties in our lives. Amen.

Reading

Mark 14:32–42

Think about It

After the Last Supper, Jesus and His friends went to the Garden of Gethsemane. Jesus knew the most important events of His earthly ministry were about to happen. Because He knew all too well what He would face, He was troubled in His soul. Jesus turned to His Father in heaven for comfort. He prayed.

How do we know that Jesus was troubled? The passage says He told His disciples, "My soul is deeply grieved to the point of death." Jesus had all the feelings we have when we are in a tough situation. He was scared and worried. If there was an easier way, He wanted to find it.

Jesus was human as well as God. This might be hard to understand, but it means that Jesus understands us completely. He knows how we feel because He felt the same things. The suffering that Jesus went through for us was very real.

What did Jesus mean when He cried out, "Abba, Father! Everything is possible for You. Take this cup from Me. Yet not what I will, but what You will" (Mark 14:36)? Jesus knew that anything and everything is possible with God, and if God chose to, He could give us salvation another way. But this was the way God had planned. There must be a punishment for sin. Either Jesus would have to take the punishment or we would have to take it ourselves. Jesus loved us too much to let us be separated from God because of our sin. He was obedient to His heavenly Father in everything. So He paid for our sins; He laid down His life for ours.

What did Jesus do when His friends fell asleep? He understood the difficulty in staying awake so late. He also knew that the only One we can truly count on and should lean on when times are rough is God. God encourages and strengthens us with spiritual power through His Word. Sometimes He changes the situation. Sometimes He changes us. But He always stays close by our side (Joshua 1:5; Hebrews 13:5).

Are any of you facing a problem right now? Share your problems with one another. Be good friends to one another. Pray to Jesus to accept His help. He knows what it's like to be in a tough situation. You don't have to go through it alone!

131

Sing!

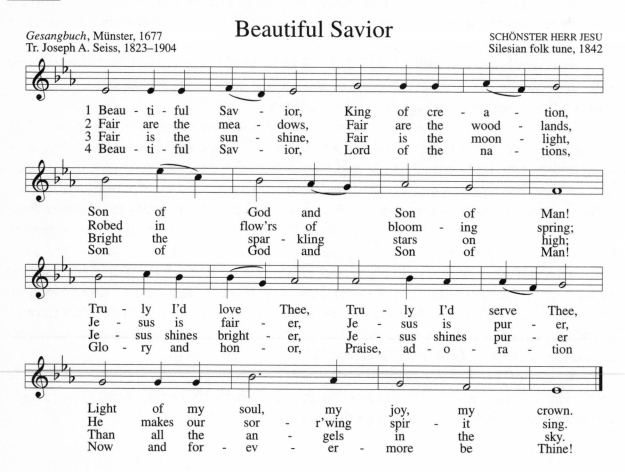

Beautiful Savior

Gesangbuch, Münster, 1677
Tr. Joseph A. Seiss, 1823–1904

SCHÖNSTER HERR JESU
Silesian folk tune, 1842

1 Beau - ti - ful Sav - ior, King of cre - a - tion,
2 Fair are the mea - dows, Fair are the wood - lands,
3 Fair is the sun - shine, Fair is the moon - light,
4 Beau - ti - ful Sav - ior, Lord of the na - tions,

Son of God and Son of Man!
Robed in flow'rs of bloom - ing spring;
Bright the spar - kling stars on high;
Son of God and Son of Man!

Tru - ly I'd love Thee, Tru - ly I'd serve Thee,
Je - sus is fair - er, Je - sus is pur - er,
Je - sus shines bright - er, Je - sus shines pur - er
Glo - ry and hon - or, Praise, ad - o - ra - tion

Light of my soul, my joy, my crown.
He makes our sor - r'wing spir - it sing.
Than all the an - gels in the sky.
Now and for - ev - er - more be Thine!

Let's Pray

Holy Lord, Jesus Christ, help us follow Your example, turning to God our Father whenever problems come into our lives. It is comforting to know You will always be besides us and will guide us to do the right thing. Amen.

Activity Time

Place an orange egg in your basket. Orange is for the twilight of the night sky while Jesus prayed alone to our Father in heaven.

Wednesday of Holy Week

Let's Pray

Jesus, we praise You for who You are: God's beloved Son. We praise You for Your love for us that caused You to hold back Your angels that night in the garden. Amen.

Reading

Matthew 26:47–56

Think about It

It was under the cover of night that they came to get Jesus. They knew the people of the city loved Him and believed He was sent from God. So to avoid a fight in the city streets, the leaders and their soldiers thought they would outsmart Jesus and steal Him away at night. They thought they were in control of the situation, but they never were. God's plan was played out like a drama and they were merely following their roles. Even in all the confusion, Jesus never forgot who He was and what He had come to do.

At the Passover supper, Jesus warned His followers that one of them would betray Him. *Who betrayed Him and how did he do it?* Betrayal is a violation of a friendship. It is doing something harmful to a friend on purpose. Judas was one of Jesus' close friends; he even chose a kiss as a signal so the soldiers would know who to capture. They had traveled together for three years—eating, sleeping, walking, and serving God together. Now His friend had turned Him over to be arrested by the temple guards. *How would you feel if your best friend hurt you like this?*

How did Jesus' other friends react when the soldiers reached out to take Him? The Bible says that at least one of them reacted in anger. Peter jumped to action and attacked one of the soldiers, cutting off his ear. *What was Jesus' response to this (Luke 23:51)?* Jesus healed the soldier's ear immediately and called for order. He knew there was no need for bloodshed that night. Then He reminded the leaders and soldiers that He was in their hands because He wanted to be, not because they had outsmarted Him. There were legions of angels ready to fight for Him should He ask them. This arrest did not serve man's purpose; it served God's.

Jesus didn't act like a scared prisoner at all. *Instead, what did He say to the leaders and soldiers who arrested Him (verses 55–56)?* Jesus scolded them and asked why they came to the garden at night for Him when He openly taught in the temple courts each day. Then Jesus told them why they did it that way—they were making God's prophecies come true. Jesus wasn't afraid of men and what they could do to Him; He was on God's mission. He never forgot it.

Sing!

I Am Trusting You, Lord Jesus

Frances R. Havergal, 1836–79, alt.

STEPHANOS
Henry W. Baker, 1821–77

1 I am trust - ing You, Lord Je - sus, Trust - ing on - ly You;
2 I am trust - ing You for par - don; At Your feet I bow,
3 I am trust - ing You for cleans - ing In the crim - son flood;
4 I am trust - ing You to guide me; You a - lone shall lead,

Trust - ing You for full sal - va - tion, Free and true.
For Your grace and ten - der mer - cy Trust - ing now.
Trust - ing You to make me ho - ly By Your blood.
Ev - 'ry day and hour sup - ply - ing All my need.

5 I am trusting You for power;
   You can never fail.
Words which You Yourself shall give me
   Must prevail.

6 I am trusting You, Lord Jesus;
   Never let me fall.
I am trusting You forever
   And for all.

Let's Pray

We praise You, Lord Jesus, because things aren't always what they seem. Looking on the outside, Your arrest was a sad and frightening time for everyone except You. You knew it was the road to our salvation. Your love comes shining through to us even now, over 2000 years later. We thank You from the bottom of our hearts! Amen.

Activity Time

Place a purple egg in your Easter basket. Purple is for Jesus' kingly authority. He didn't lose His authority to a group of misguided leaders and soldiers—He laid it down for our sake.

Thursday of Holy Week

Let's Pray

We thank You, dear Lord Jesus, for Your faithfulness to us. You have never failed or betrayed us. You are so good. We are so grateful. Amen.

Reading

Mark 14:66–72

Think about It

Yesterday, we discussed how Judas betrayed Jesus to the chief priests and leaders. We watched as he used a kiss to seal the deal. But the betrayal told in this Bible passage is different. It may have been even more painful for both Jesus and the betrayer—Peter. Peter did not intentionally deny Jesus. In fact, he was one of the few disciples to follow the soldiers as they took Jesus away. Peter didn't set out to reject his Lord; he just slid into it and caught himself only after it was too late. The deed was done.

What was Peter thinking about when he kept saying he didn't know Jesus? Peter was in the courtyard of the temple, surrounded by guards, soldiers, and others loyal to the people who had just arrested Jesus. He was very upset by what had happened. Peter probably wondered what would happen to him and the other disciples. He may have wondered if they would be arrested too. And he was afraid. In those days, prisoners were treated very badly. They were beaten, hurt, and sometimes even killed.

Did Peter's betrayal end his friendship with Jesus? Thankfully, no, it didn't. Jesus forgives every sin. Even when the sin is a friend's betrayal. As soon as Peter said, "I don't know Him!" he knew what he had done and was very, very sorry for it. The weight of his betrayal caused him a lot of pain. *Have you ever felt sorry for saying something hurtful as soon as you said it?* Words can't be taken back. That is why the Bible tells us to be careful about how we speak (Ephesians 5:19; Colossians 3:17; James 3:2–12).

Read John 21:1–19 and tell how Jesus showed Peter he was forgiven. After Jesus' resurrection, He made a special breakfast for Peter on the beach. While they talked and ate together, Jesus forgave Peter, giving him a new job to do. While Jesus will not like our actions when we hurt Him by our thoughts, actions, or words, He will always love us and forgive us. We can always come back to Him and receive forgiveness. The Bible says nothing separates us from the love of God that is in Christ Jesus, our Lord (Romans 8:39).

Let's Pray

Lord Jesus, we are thankful that nothing can stay between You and us and keep us from Your love. Help us to faithfully live for You, although we sometimes fail. Please forgive us and help us remember that Your love lasts forever. In Your name. Amen.

Activity Time

Place the black egg in the basket. Black helps us remember the sin that fills our heart without Jesus. If Peter, one of Jesus' best friends, could betray Him, we could too.

Sing!

Stand Up, Stand Up for Jesus

George Duffield, 1818–88, alt.

George J. Webb, 1803–87

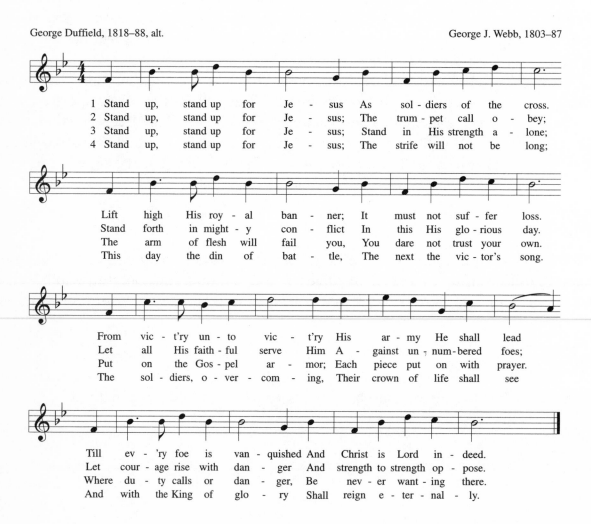

1 Stand up, stand up for Je - sus As sol - diers of the cross.
2 Stand up, stand up for Je - sus; The trum - pet call o - bey;
3 Stand up, stand up for Je - sus; Stand in His strength a - lone;
4 Stand up, stand up for Je - sus; The strife will not be long;

Lift high His roy - al ban - ner; It must not suf - fer loss.
Stand forth in might - y con - flict In this His glo - rious day.
The arm of flesh will fail you, You dare not trust your own.
This day the din of bat - tle, The next the vic - tor's song.

From vic - t'ry un - to vic - t'ry His ar - my He shall lead
Let all His faith - ful serve Him A - gainst un - num - bered foes;
Put on the Gos - pel ar - mor; Each piece put on with prayer.
The sol - diers, o - ver - com - ing, Their crown of life shall see

Till ev - 'ry foe is van - quished And Christ is Lord in - deed.
Let cour - age rise with dan - ger And strength to strength op - pose.
Where du - ty calls or dan - ger, Be nev - er want - ing there.
And with the King of glo - ry Shall reign e - ter - nal - ly.

Good Friday

It was now about the sixth hour,
and darkness came over
the whole land
until the ninth hour,
for the sun stopped shining.
Luke 23:44—45a

Let's Pray

Dear Lord Jesus, remind us today of the greatest sacrifice ever made—Your death for us. We are so very thankful for it and for Your love that never ends. Amen.

Reading

John 19:16–37

Think about It

It was a day like no other. It was the worst day in history. It was the greatest day in history. It was the day Jesus Christ became our Savior. He was nailed to a rough wooden cross. It wasn't like the shiny gold crosses we see today, but an ugly and roughly cut log. He died there to set us free from the sin that caught and held all the people of the world since Adam and Eve. The day stayed dark and gloomy as Jesus hung from that cruel cross. His death did not come easily. We were bought with a very great price.

There were many Old Testament prophecies foretelling what Jesus would do and what would happen to Him. Read Psalm 22:18 and John 19:23–24. The soldiers had no idea they were under God's direction. At a crucifixion, the soldiers in charge simply took anything they wanted from the person who was executed. They made fun of him and treated him badly. God foretold what would happen on Good Friday long before it did so we would know it was all a part of His plan. God allowed Jesus to be treated this way. Jesus suffered so we would not have to.

What was the first thing Jesus did while hanging on the cross? Jesus always thought of His loved ones first. In this passage, He wanted to make sure someone would take care of Mary, His mother. In those days, women usually did not live by themselves; they lived within a family. Jesus made sure Mary would have a family to care for her after He died. *Isn't His love awesome?* Even while He was in terrible pain on the cross, He cared for her!

Death on a cross came slowly; it took hours or even days for the person to die. The physical pain was worse than any of us can imagine. There were also hurtful words that came from the soldiers and others in the crowd. But the worst pain was in being totally alone and separated from God's love. Jesus' suffering had a reason. It brought us peace with God. There is no greater love in all the world than the love Jesus has for you and for me.

Why did Jesus say "It is finished"? Because Jesus is God, He knew the exact moment when our salvation was paid in full. He knew when all the prophecies about Him were fulfilled. He knew how much suffering was necessary. He was in charge the whole time. Those Roman soldiers didn't take His life; He gave it for us (John 15:13).

Why do we call the day Jesus died "Good" Friday? What happened to Jesus and the pain He went through wasn't good. But what has happened to us because of it is good. In fact it is wonderful! He died so we could be free from sin and death (Galatians 5:1).

Jesus died so we might have new life; He called it abundant life. That abundant life is living in a daily friendship with God, loving Him, obeying Him, and serving Him. It is knowing the warmth of His love, grace, and forgiveness each and every day. We are loved with an everlasting love and Good Friday showed us just how much love that is.

Sing!

Just as I Am

Charlotte Elliott, 1789–1871

WOODWORTH
William B. Bradbury, 1816–68

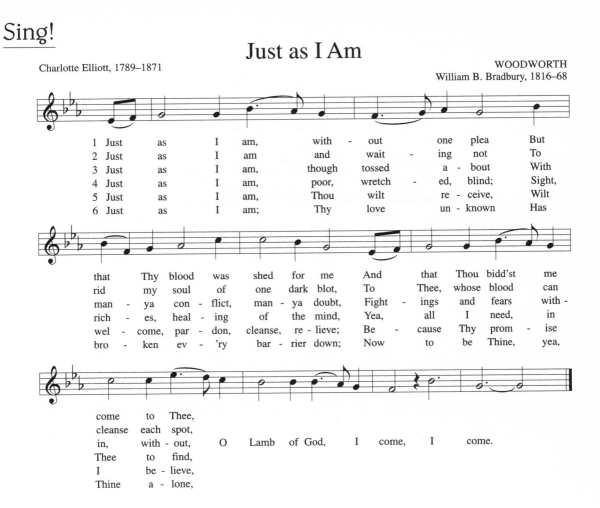

1 Just as I am, with - out one plea But
2 Just as I am and wait - ing not To
3 Just as I am, though tossed a - bout With
4 Just as I am, poor, wretch - ed, blind; Sight,
5 Just as I am, Thou wilt re - ceive, Wilt
6 Just as I am; Thy love un - known Has

that Thy blood was shed for me And that Thou bidd'st me
rid my soul of one dark blot, To Thee, whose blood can
man - ya con - flict, man - ya doubt, Fight - ings and fears with -
rich - es, heal - ing of the mind, Yea, all I need, in
wel - come, par - don, cleanse, re - lieve; Be - cause Thy prom - ise
bro - ken ev - 'ry bar - rier down; Now to be Thine, yea,

come to Thee,
cleanse each spot,
in, with - out, O Lamb of God, I come, I come.
Thee to find,
I be - lieve,
Thine a - lone,

Let's Pray

Lord Jesus, we are sorry for the sins that sent You to the cross. We thank You for saving us, since we couldn't save ourselves. Thank You for the gift of Your grace and forgiveness. Help us live the abundant life You promised to those who believe in You. Thank You, Lord. Amen.

Activity Time

Place the red egg in your Easter basket. The color red reminds us of the blood that was shed for our sins. Jesus' red blood makes us white as snow.

Holy Saturday

> ...He rolled a big stone in front of the entrance to the tomb and went away.
>
> Matthew 27:60b

Let's Pray

Thank You, Jesus, that death and sin have no power over us now. We are free in Your name. Help us to always have faith in You. Amen.

Reading

Luke 23:50–56; Romans 6:8–10; and 1 Corinthians 15:55–58

Think about It

Jesus was buried in Joseph of Arimathea's grave. It had to be done quickly because the Sabbath was beginning and the Jewish people were not supposed to do work of any kind on the Sabbath. The suffering was over. The sins of the entire world were paid for. The evil that came into the world when Adam and Eve disobeyed God had no power because people were no longer separated from God.

Does Jesus have to die over and over again (Romans 6:9)? Unlike the lamb offerings of the Old Testament that were needed over and over again, Jesus had to die only once for our sins. He is the perfect Lamb of God. His sacrifice gave us a new friendship with God that is never broken. Before we were separated from Him, now we are His beloved children.

What does "the sting of death is sin" mean (1 Corinthians 15:56)? It is because of sin that death came into the world. The payment or punishment for our sins is death (Romans 6:23). When Jesus defeated sin on the cross, He gave us eternal life as a gift.

Since Jesus defeated death, why do people still die? We still have to live with the consequences of Adam and Eve's sin. When they disobeyed God, He made them leave the Garden of Eden. Imagine you and your brother playing catch in the living room even after your mom told you not to. Your throw goes wild and breaks a lamp. You can ask for and receive forgiveness, but that doesn't fix the lamp.

Instead of our living forever here on earth, Jesus has made us a wonderful new home in heaven. But for us to get there, we must leave our earthly bodies. Although we must die physically, thanks to Jesus we will never die spiritually. If we have believed in Him while on earth, we will be with Him forever in heaven. It's a done deal.

Since Jesus paid for our sins, does that mean we will never do anything wrong? As long as we are on this earth we will sin. Maybe it will be a sin that we speak or think or do. This happens when we act only for ourselves and do not follow God's Word. Maybe it will be something we leave undone, kind words or actions we could have done for others but did not. We sin every day in one way or another. It is important to ask God to forgive our sins each day (James 1:9). He always will. He will also give us the strength and the grace to keep trying to live lives that are obedient and pleasing to Him.

Let's Pray

You are all-powerful, Jesus. Your victory over sin and death gives us freedom to follow You, to serve You, and to love You. Thank You, Jesus, for first loving us. Thank You for helping us out of the deep problems our sins cause. Amen.

Sing!

Amazing Grace

John Newton, 1725–1807, alt.

NEW BRITAIN
J. Carrell and D. Clayton, *Virginia Harmony*, 1831

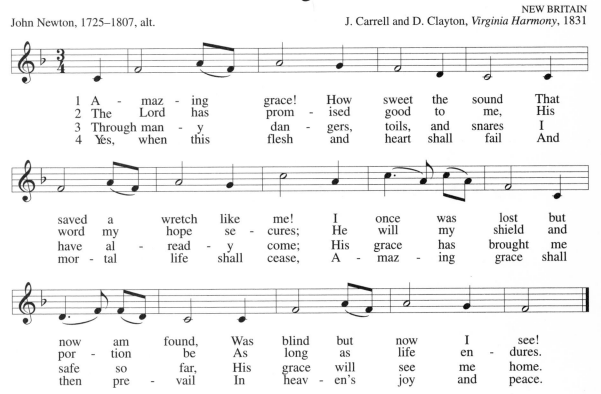

1 A - maz - ing grace! How sweet the sound That
2 The Lord has prom - ised good to me, His
3 Through man - y dan - gers, toils, and snares I
4 Yes, when this flesh and heart shall fail And

saved a wretch like me! I once was lost but
word my hope se - cures; He will my shield and
have al - read - y come; His grace has brought me
mor - tal life shall cease, A - maz - ing grace shall

now am found, Was blind but now I see!
por - tion be As long as life en - dures.
safe so far, His grace will see me home.
then pre - vail In heav - en's joy and peace.

Activity Time

Place a green egg in your Easter basket. Green stands for the eternal life that is yours when you believe in Jesus Christ, God's only Son.

145

Easter Sunday: Rejoicing for He Has Risen Indeed!

"Why do you look for the living among the dead? He is not here; He has risen!" Luke 24:5—6

Let's Pray

Alleluia! We praise You, our risen Lord, Jesus Christ! Along with the apostle Thomas, we say, "my Lord and my God." You have risen indeed, and we rejoice. Amen.

Reading

Matthew 28:1–10

Think about It

When the Sabbath was over, the women came back to the tomb to get Jesus' body ready for burial. They had put Him in the tomb quickly on Friday before the Sabbath began. Their hearts were filled with sorrow. They were going to do a job that is difficult to do at any time, but it was especially hard this time. All their hopes and dreams about who Jesus was and what He would do were destroyed. They didn't know what to think.

But what the women found at the tomb left them thrilled and excited—an angel, an empty tomb, and their Lord alive and well. It was a miraculous ending to the greatest story ever told.

Scripture says that an angel of the Lord rolled away the huge stone covering the tomb. *Jesus didn't need the stone moved to get out of the tomb, so why did it need to be rolled away?*

146

He is God; He can do anything. People needed the stone rolled away. It showed them that Jesus wasn't there. He is alive.

If you were a guard, what would you have thought? These guards were responsible for making sure nothing happened to Jesus' body. It was an important job, and if they didn't do it, they would get into big trouble, maybe even be put to death. When the earthquake rumbled and the angel appeared, they weren't just afraid—they were terrified. The Bible says they shook and were like dead men. They couldn't talk or run or use their spears. All they could do was watch God's power in action.

What did the angel tell the women? The angel told them not to be afraid. They didn't have anything to fear like the guards did. In fact the angel had wonderful, life-changing news for them. He told them to look for themselves at the place Jesus was laid; He wasn't there. Jesus had risen. The angel urged them to run quickly and tell the disciples.

Who greeted the two Marys as they set out to obey the angel's command? None other than the Lord Jesus Himself. What a miracle! Now joy filled their hearts to bursting. Doubt and grief were gone. Jesus wasn't dead. Hope was not lost. He fought against sin and death and Satan, and He won. Jesus is our Lord and Savior.

Parents: He has risen!

Children: He has risen indeed!

Let's Pray

Jesus, our dear Lord and Savior, our hearts are filled with joy now just as the two Marys' hearts were. All of our hope is in You, Lord. You are the risen Lord who saves us from our sins. We love You. We thank You. We worship You. Amen.

Activity Time

Is He living and reigning as your King today? Place a gold egg in your Easter basket. Gold is the most precious of minerals. Your salvation was bought with a price and will last forever.

Sing!

Jesus Christ Is Risen Today

Latin carol, 14th cent., sts. 1–3
Charles Wesley, 1707–88, st. 4
Tr. *Lyra Davidica*, London, 1708, sts. 1–3

Lyra Davidica, London, 1708

1 Je - sus Christ is ris'n to - day,
2 Hymns of praise then let us sing,
3 But the pains which He en - dured,
4 Sing we to our God a - bove,

Al - le - lu - ia!

Our tri - um - phant ho - ly day,
Un - to Christ, our heav'n - ly king,
Our sal - va - tion have pro - cured;
Praise e - ter - nal as His love;

Al - le - lu - ia!

Who did once up - on the cross,
Who en - dured the cross and grave,
Now a - bove the sky He's king,
Praise Him, all you heav'n - ly host,

Al - le - lu - ia!

Suf - fer to re - deem our loss.
Sin - ners to re - deem and save.
Where the an - gels ev - er sing.
Fa - ther, Son, and Ho - ly Ghost.

Al - le - lu - ia!

Ideas for Fasting

The following ideas can be done for the entire period of Lent or just a part of it. Your family can have a regular fast day and do the same fast each week or choose a different fast every week. Consider having each person in your family choose an individual fast, something that is a personal sacrifice for them.

If your family has never fasted, start with something easy and keep it short. Do not engage an infant, toddler, or preschooler in a food fast, for example. They are too young to understand or benefit from its meaning. A good alternative might be substituting a simple meal of bread and milk for a regular meal.

Remember to spend extra time praying, reading God's Word, and worshiping Him during the fast. Don't allow your children to grumble about what they are fasting from. Instead, encourage them to turn their eyes toward Jesus and all He does for us.

1. Fast from a meal and donate the money to a food bank or homeless shelter. This could be done one time or as a weekly observance during Lent. Use the meal time to pray and worship together.

2. Fast from sweet things

3. Fast from red meat.

4. Fast from cooked food. Try to prepare a nutritious meal without using the stove, oven, or microwave. Rejoice in God's bountiful fresh food supply.

5. Fast from video games.

6. Fast from TV altogether or just from specific television shows.

7. Fast from allowance money. For parents that could include money you would normally spend on a cup of coffee or soda during the day. Collect the money and give it instead to a missionary.

8. Fast from loud music. Try playing only soothing, soft music.

9. Fast from certain habits like biting your fingernails, drumming your nails on the table, or "you fill in the blank."

10. Fast from late nights.

11. Fast from sleeping in.

12. Fast from driving a car for a day. Can your family get around for a day without it?

13. Fast from the telephone. If you're brave enough, turn off the answering machine too! (If you're not, at least don't check it until the next day.)

14. Fast from the computer—no games, no Internet, no e-mail.

15. Fast from complaining. See if your family can speak only words of blessing and encouragement to one another.

16. Fast from criticizing, judging, or blaming. This is very similar to the fast from complaining, but one that your kids will find challenging. Read and discuss Scriptures on judging and critical spirits. You can even fine the occasional slip and donate that money to a charity or add it to your offerings during the next worship service.

17. Fast from purchasing non-essential items. Buy only items your family genuinely needs during this period. Resist the temptation to buy impulse items or things your family can do without. A fast like this should last until the family members feel its pinch a little. Talk about the differences between needing and wanting.

18. Fast from the comforts of life. Try spending a day without using conveniences like electronic devices or appliances. Yes, that means—no TV, telephone, computer, microwave, etc.! Limit the kids to one or two store-bought playthings. Spend the day as simply as you can.

19. Fast from noise. Try to fast from needless talking, yelling, and general noise-making. Reflect on Jesus' times of withdrawing to be alone with the Father. This kind of fast may work best if all family members go in their rooms for a specific amount of time with instructions to spend the time thinking, praying, or reading God's Word.

20. Sorry kids, no fasting from homework!

Teaching Your Children about the Resurrection

Note: these activities take a little more planning and preparation time, but the kids will love them and learn more about resurrection.

Force Bloom a Bulb

(Daffodils, crocus, tulips, and hyacinths work well for this.) Use a flowerpot that is at least twice as tall as your bulbs and large enough to hold three or four bulbs. Mix the potting soil with bone meal or bulb fertilizer to give the bulbs a healthy start. Partially fill the pot with the soil.

Place the bulbs on the soil. The growing tip of the bulb should reach the top of the pot. The bulbs should be placed close together but should not touch other bulbs or the sides of the pot. Sprinkle more soil over the bulbs until only the tips are showing.

Water the soil and keep it moist. Put the container in a cool, dark place like a basement, cool closet, or refrigerator. Continue to moisten the soil. When stems are about two inches high, move the pot to a warm, sunny place, and the bulbs will continue to grow and bloom.

This process takes about 12 weeks, so you should to begin 10 to 12 weeks before Ash Wednesday.

Have a Butterfly Farm

Purchase a butterfly kit from a mail-order company or online source at the beginning of Lent. As a family, take care of the caterpillars, then watch as they build their cocoons and wait until the beautiful butterflies appear. Later you can set them free. This is an apt lesson on life, "death," resurrection, and ascension.

Grow Flowers for Your Summer Garden

Try growing summer flowers, such as marigolds or snapdragons, from seeds. Time your planting so you will begin to have blooms at Easter. Discuss together all the things a flower needs to bloom. First it must be attached to a plant (see John 15). It must be planted into good soil and receive the right amounts of sunshine and water. Only then will the seeds sprout and grow into something beautiful.

Watch Eggs Hatch into Baby Chicks

Depending where you live, see if you can find a farm, pet store, or children's museum with chicken eggs your family could visit regularly to watch until they hatch.

Watch Tadpoles Develop into Frogs

Depending where you live, visit a pond and look for frog eggs. Make several return trips, watching for the tadpoles and finally the young frogs. Talk about your child's life, how it is now and how it will change as she or he grows up. Talk about how all our lives change as we grow older until they are completed and we finally go to our eternal home in heaven.

Hide It in Your Heart: Memory Verses for Lent

Here are some Scripture verses you and your family may choose to memorize during this Lenten season.

Beginning of Lent

Matthew 3:17 And a voice from heaven said, "This is My Son, whom I love; with Him I am well pleased."

Matthew 4:4 Jesus answered, "It is written: 'Man does not live on bread alone, but on every word that comes from the mouth of God.'"

Hebrews 4:14 Therefore, since we have a great high priest who has gone through the heavens, Jesus the Son of God, let us hold firmly to the faith we profess.

Hebrews 4:16 Let us then approach the throne of grace with confidence, so that we may receive mercy and find grace to help us in our time of need.

Second Week of Lent

Isaiah 53:3a He was despised and rejected by men, a man of sorrows, and familiar with suffering.

Luke 2:40 And the child grew and became strong; He was filled with wisdom, and the grace of God was upon Him.

John 1:1 In the beginning was the Word, and the Word was with God, and the Word was God.

John 1:29 The next day John saw Jesus coming toward him and said, "Look, the Lamb of God, who takes away the sin of the world."

John 3:16 "For God so loved the world that He gave His one and only Son, that whoever believes in Him shall not perish but have eternal life."

Third Week of Lent

Matthew 22:37 Jesus replied: "Love the Lord your God with all your heart and with all your soul and with all your mind."

Matthew 22:38 "And the second is like it: 'Love your neighbor as yourself.'"

John 6:35 Then Jesus declared, "I am the bread of life. He who comes to Me will never go hungry, and he who believes in Me will never be thirsty."

John 11:25 Jesus said to her, "I am the resurrection and the life. He who believes in Me will live, even though he dies."

John 14:6 Jesus answered, "I am the way and the truth and the life. No one comes to the Father except through Me."

Fourth Week of Lent

Matthew 4:19 "Come, follow Me," Jesus said, "and I will make you fishers of men."

John: 20:28 Thomas said to Him, "My Lord and my God!"

2 Corinthians 9:6 Whoever sows sparingly will also reap sparingly, and whoever sows generously will also reap generously.

2 Corinthians 9:7 God loves a cheerful giver.

Fifth Week of Lent

Matthew 16:24 "If anyone would come after Me. He must deny himself and take up his cross and follow Me."

Matthew 22:37–38 Jesus replied, "Love the Lord your God with all your heart and with all your soul and with all your mind. This is the first and greatest commandment."

Matthew 28:19 "Therefore go and make disciples of all nations, baptizing them in the name of the Father and of the Son and the Holy Spirit."

Luke 5:10b "Don't be afraid; from now on you will catch men."

John 8:31–32 "If you hold to My teaching, you are really My disciples. Then you will know the truth, and the truth will set you free."

Galatians 5:22 But the fruit of the Spirit is love, joy, peace, patience, kindness, goodness, faithfulness, gentleness and self-control. Against such things there is no law.

Sixth Week of Lent

Matthew 22:39 "And the second is like it: 'Love your neighbor as yourself.'"

Matthew 25:40 "The King will reply, 'I tell you the truth, whatever you did for one of the least of these brothers of Mine, you did for Me.'"

Mark 10:45 "For even the Son of man did not come to be served, but to serve, and to give His life as a ransom for many."

Luke 6:35a "But love your enemies, do good to them, and lend to them without expecting to get anything back."

Luke 6:36 "Be merciful, just as your Father is merciful."

Galatians 6:9 Let us not become weary in doing good, for at the proper time we will reap a harvest if we do not give up.

Holy Week

Matthew 26:53 "Do you think I cannot call on My Father, and He will at once put at My disposal more that twelve legions of angels?"

Matthew 28:5–6 Do not be afraid, for I know that you are looking for Jesus, who was crucified. He is not here; He has risen, just as He said.

Romans 6:11 In the same way, count yourselves dead to sin but alive to God in Christ Jesus.

1 Corinthians 15:55–57 Where, O death, is your victory? Where, O death, is your sting? The sting of death is sin, and the power of sin is the law. But thanks be to God. He gives us the victory through our Lord Jesus Christ.

Ephesians 2:8–9 For it is by grace you have been saved, through faith—and this not from yourselves, it is the gift of God—not by works, so no one can boast.

Hymn Index

Unless otherwise noted, the hymn texts and settings in this book are in the public domain.

A Note from the Author

Thank you for the privilege of sharing these family times with you. As my own family gathered around our table, we thought of you and prayed that you would be touched by the incredible love of Jesus during this holy season.

May you and yours always seek His face and be warmed in the light of His love.

Kimberly Ingalls Reese